the food of
korea

63 Simple and Delicious Recipes
from the Land of the Morning Calm

by Injoo Chun, Jaewoon Lee and Youngran Baek
photos by Masano Kawana
Styling by Christina Ong and Kim Kyung Mi

PERIPLUS EDITIONS
Singapore • Hong Kong • Indonesia

Published by Periplus Editions (HK) Ltd. with editorial offices at and 61 Tai Seng Avenue, #02-12, Singapore 534167

ISBN 978-0-7946-0503-2
Previously published as Authentic Recipes from Korea ISBN 0-7946-0287-8

Distributed by

North America, Latin America & Europe
Tuttle Publishing, 364 Innovation Drive
North Clarendon, VT 05759-9436 U.S.A.
Tel: 1 (802) 773-8930; Fax: 1 (802) 773-6993
info@tuttlepublishing.com
www.tuttlepublishing.com

Japan
Tuttle Publishing, Yaekari Building, 3rd Floor
5-4-12 Osaki, Shinagawa-ku, Tokyo 141 0032
Tel: (81) 03 5437-0171; Fax: (81) 03 5437-0755
tuttle-sales@gol.com

Asia Pacific
Berkeley Books Pte Ltd.
61 Tai Seng Avenue, #02-12
Singapore 534167
Tel: (65) 6280-1330; Fax: (65) 6280-6290
inquiries@periplus.com.sg
www.periplus.com

Photo Credits: All photography by Masano Kawana.
Additional photos by Craig J. Brown (pages 4, 7, 11–12, 17 top).
Food Consultant: Mrs Lee Soo Young
All recipes were tested in the Periplus Test Kitchen.

10 09 08
6 5 4 3 2

Printed in Hong Kong

Contents

Food in Korea

Geography, climate and history have all shaped Korea's distinctive cuisine

The Korean peninsula juts out like a spur from the Asian mainland, just below Manchuria in northeastern China and eastern Siberia. Approximately the size of the United Kingdom, it stretches 620 miles (1,000 kilometers) north to south, but is only 135 miles (216 kilometers) east to west at its narrowest point. To the west lies the Yellow Sea and China; to the east the East Sea and Japan. Scattered off the jagged coastline are some 3,000 islands.

Apart from the encircling sea, Korea is a land of mountains. An enduring image of this Land of Morning Calm, as it has become known, is of wave upon wave of blue mountains, their peaks rising through the morning mist. Only 20 percent of the country consists of arable land, and of this, a large proportion is represented by the rice-growing Honam plain in southwest Korea. The east coast, ribbed by the magnificent Diamond Mountains, falls abruptly to the East Sea. The west coast is riddled with shallow, narrow inlets that experience large tidal changes. Between these coasts the peninsula is ribboned with swift-flowing rivers originating in the mountains.

In addition to water, the country is rich in forests. An extensive reforestation program began after the Korean War and now the mountain parks are full of juniper, bamboo, willow, red maples, and flowering fruit and nut trees such as apricot, pear, peach, plum, cherry, persimmon, chestnut, walnut, gingko and pine nut. Autumn in the Sorak mountains off the east coast, or spring at Kyongju, ancient capital of unified Korea, brings a marvel of foliage in varying hues.

Korea has four distinct seasons: spring and autumn are temperate, winter and summer verge on the extremes. Winter is particularly cold, with temperatures dropping to 24°F (-5°C) or less, and often lasts from November until late March. This climate, in combination with the mountainous interior, has given Koreans an appetite for hearty, stimulating food—meats and soups are cooked with chilies, garlic, ginseng, and many medicinal vegetables, berries and nuts—which helps to keep out the cold and produce energy. At the same time, the four seasons have guaranteed the Koreans a steady flow of seasonal produce. The lowland fields provide excellent grains and vegetables, while the uplands grow wild and cultivated mushrooms, roots and greens. The surrounding seas produce a host of fish, seafood, seaweed and crustaceans. However, it is the sense of food as medicine and long-term protection that has governed the evolution of the Korean diet. Even raw fish sashimi is given extra vitality by being seasoned with red chili. Most meals are served with a gruel or a soup, as well as the ubiquitous, fortifying kimchi and a range of veg-etarian side dishes collectively known as *namul*, which are delicately seasoned with soy, sesame and garlic.

Koreans often look to herbal remedies for illnesses, the result of their grounding in Chinese medical belief about the yin-yang balance of the body and the cooling-warming properties of certain foods. The most common medicinal foods used in cooking are dried persimmon, dried red dates, pine seeds, chestnut, gingko, tangerine and ginseng. The saponin in garlic, which Koreans often eat raw, wrapped in a lettuce leaf around barbecued meat, is said to cleanse the blood and aid digestion. Chicken and pork are considered the first steps to obesity, so are largely avoided. Nuts are supposed to be good for pregnancy as well as the skin; dried red dates and bellflower root for coughs and colds and raw potato juice for an upset stomach, while dried pollack with bean sprouts and tofu is said to be good for hangovers.

Much of Korean history was characterized by the struggle between the supporters of Buddhism and Confucianism for control of the system of patronage; this consequently also greatly influenced the food. The Silla Kingdom, based on Kyongju, united the Korean nation for the first time in the 7th century, giving birth to a long period of Buddhist culture. This culture continued to flourish into the Koryo Dynasty (AD 935–1368). However, although Koryo patronized Buddhism and the monks played an important role in national affairs, the Koryo kings also adopted Confucian-style government bureaucracy and civil service examinations from China. By the time Genghis Khan's Mongol alliance invaded Korea in 1231, the Koryo court had become torn between Confucian reform and the age-old Buddhist cultural heritage. A treaty made with China in 1279 gave Koryo semi-autonomy but required Korean princes to reside in the new Mongol capital at Beijing; they also had to marry Mongol princesses.

When the Ming Dynasty was established in China in 1368, and the Mongols were driven out, Koryo looked like the next prize on the list. However, the invading armies of the Ming Chinese were driven back by Yi Sog-gye, a fiery Korean commander who deposed the king of Koryo and invoked the Mandate of Heaven to establish his own Yi Dynasty.

The Yi Dynasty lasted over 500 years and ended only with the annexation of Korea by Japan in 1910. Yi's first king was wily enough to reestablish tributary relations with China and to also adopt Confucianism as the state creed, renaming his kingdom Chosun, after China's ancient name for Korea.

LEFT: A fishing village on Ulleungdo Island, prized for its seasonal fish and cuttlefish. The quality of their seafood is so fresh and well known that it is exported to countries such as Japan and the US.

From then onwards, Confucianism steadily replaced Buddhism in national life; and in effect, Buddhism was banished to Korea's mountain temples. There, close to the forests and mountain streams, Buddhist monks continued to study the scriptures. They also developed a "mountain cuisine" that has become the foundation of Korean cooking today. For example, meat, which is forbidden to the Buddhist monk, and anything that is strong smelling, such as garlic and spring onion, did not feature in temple cuisine. While modern Korean Buddhism is not so rigid about garlic, this cuisine has retained its traditional dependence on roots, grasses and herbs. Today, the visitor to any temples from Seoraksan in the northeast to Chirisan in the south is greeted by piles of mushrooms, roots and medicinal herbs on sale at the entrance. A typical temple meal consists of soup, rice and *namul*, vegetable dishes, in which the vegetables are gathered from the woods and the hills.

The collected roots and grasses are then prepared simply with soy sauce, crushed garlic, sesame seeds, sesame oil and seasonings. The preparation of *namul* varies from region to region, but the dishes are exactly the same as the side dishes of *namul* that accompany family and restaurant meals in Korean cities and towns, consisting of appetizers of shepherd's purse, mugwort, parsley and sow thistle; *namul* of wild aster, bracken, royal fern, marsh plant, day lily, aralia roots and bellflower, to name just a few.

Other stalwarts of the Korean table originate from the mountains, too, such as vegetable pancakes or *jeon*, which are usually filled with lentils or leeks and are sometimes fashioned in the shape of a flower.

The Culinary Tour of the Peninsula

Kyonggido Province surrounding Seoul offers rice and grain farmlands, vegetables from the eastern mountains and seafood from the Yellow Sea. Simple fare, served in generous, rather unspicy portions, include beef rib soup (*galbitang*), made of well-marbled short ribs boiled for as long as it takes to draw out the marrow; beef stock soup (*gomtang*), boiled with beef entrails and radishes; and the springtime shepherd's purse soup (*naengiguk*), boiled with soybean paste, hot chili paste and clams.

By contrast, the rugged Kangwondo Province to the east provides abundant seafood due to the crossing of warm and cold currents in the East Sea. The region is mountainous, and offers many kinds of cereals, corn and potatoes. The fare is unsophisticated but healthy, including stuffed squid (*ojingoh sundae*) with bean curd and vegetables from tiny Ulleungdo Island and mudfish stew (*chuohtang*), made with mudfish, potatoes, leeks and mushrooms; fried potato pancakes (*gamjajeon*), mixed with chopped leeks, spring onions and green chilies, which is a speciality of the snowy Seoraksan and Odaesan national parks; and cold buckwheat noodles (*memil makguksu*) at Chuncheon, the provincial capital, delicately spiced with kimchi juice and cold beef stock.

Chungcheong-do Province is divided between its south coast and a northern landlocked part. South Chungcheong harvests sumptuous marine products from plentiful fishing grounds in the Yellow Sea, while North Chungcheong produces many kinds of mountain vegetables. Delicacies, which are mainly mild and savory, include Bibimbap, boiled rice with assorted mountain vegetables and mushrooms picked from Mount Songni (see page 84 for Bibimbap recipe); acorn jelly (*dotorimuk*) with acorn pancakes and cold acorn noodles as variations; grilled todok (*deodeok gui*), a pounded mountain root seasoned with red pepper paste sauce and grilled on a griddle; and pickled crabs (*kkogejang*) marinated in soy sauce, mixed with red chili, garlic and sesame oil.

Kyonsangdo, centered around the southeastern industrial city of Taegu, the port city of Pusan and the ancient capital of Kyongju, produces abundant crops and marine products all year round. The hot and salty dishes include Taegu soup (*taegutang*), in which beef is cooked with Chinese cabbage, bracken and spring onion; large clam gruel (*daehap juk*), boiled with sticky rice, dried red dates and ginseng; steamed big-mouth fish (*agutchim*), fished from the port of Masan and dried, seasoned, and steamed with watercress and bean sprouts until the bones soften; and sashimi (*saengson hoe*) of sea trout, flatfish, flounder, sweetfish and greenling caught from the East and South seas and served with sour red chili paste sauce.

Pusan boasts a magnificent early morning fish market at Jagalchi, and its sashimi restaurants—striped canvas tents that are lit at night like fortune teller booths—stretch along the craggy shoreline, offering a cornucopia of raw fish, spicy sauces and *soju* (distilled wine spirit made from potato and rice).

LEFT: A quintessential ingredient, leeks are put up for auction in the market. RIGHT: A selection of *namul*, vegetable dishes, served at a restaurant in Insadong, demonstrates the wide variety of vegetarian fare in Korea—a result of the country's Buddhist heritage.

Kyongju's seasonal fruit, such as pears, apples and persimmons, together with acorn jelly and jellyfish mustard salad, form the backdrop to several colorful, bright tasting seasonal recipes.

A varied and luxurious cuisine has been developed from the sumptuous products of the fertile Honam plain and the seas lying to the south and west of the province of Jeollado. This area is famous for the large number of side dishes served at one meal—particularly in the many traditional farmhouses—and for a unique type of kimchi. But perhaps the most famous Jeollado dish is Jeonju rice hash (*Jeonju bibimbap*), the precursor of and model for all *bibimbap* dishes in Korea. Shredded beef, soybean sprouts, dried mushrooms, bellflower root and bracken are mixed with soy sauce, garlic and sesame oil, and stir-fried until brown. The ingredients are then mixed together in a large bowl, a fried egg is placed on top and a bowl of rice is upended into the mixture.

In Jeonju, five different variations of kimchi and *namul* are placed on the table, along with big green chili peppers. The rice, which is cooked in wood and iron braziers, is mixed with a dark soy and onion sauce and served with ginseng root spread with kimchi and barbecued on the grill. The dish sets the body on fire, and the best restaurant for it in Jeonju is Chungang Hoekwan.

Jeollado also offers seasoned broiled eel (*jangeo gui*), a tonic dish in hot summer weather, seasoned with red pepper paste sauce; seasoned broiled octopus (*nakchi gui*), octopus tentacles wrapped in straw and broiled; and Jeollado kimchi, a savory kimchi of rich seafood ingredients. In addition to Chinese cabbage, the ingredients used in this kimchi are Korean lettuce, mustard greens, welsh onion, radish leaves, bean sprouts, eggplant and green chili pepper.

The romantic honeymooners' island of Jeju off the southern coast has limited cultivable land but well-stocked waters. It produces mainly cereals and sweet potatoes. The straightforward nature of the inhabitants is reflected in their food, in which seasonings are used sparingly.

Local specialties include Abalone Porridge (Jeonbokjuk, see page 50), thin slices of abalone fried with sesame oil and then mixed with rice and water before being simmered in a pot and seasoned with salt (Jeju abalone used to be offered to the king as a tribute); seafood earthen-pot stew (*haemul ttukpaegi*), boiled without vegetables but enriched with clams, oysters, sea-urchin eggs and soybean paste; stone-pot boiled rice with mushrooms (*dolsot pyogo bibimbap*), consisting of rice boiled with shiitake mushrooms and mountain vegetables picked from the slopes of Mount Halla and served on a hot stone-pot; and mixed black sea bream sashimi (*jarimulhoe*), Jeju's unique black bream sliced without removing its bones and mixed with spring onion, watercress, cucumber, Chinese pepper and cold water.

But equally, no one should visit Jeju without tasting a dish of fresh oysters, plucked from the sea by Jeju's famous women oyster divers, an example of the island's rapidly vanishing matriarchal society. Jeju also grows oranges and raises its own herds of cattle.

Finally, Seoul, the capital of Korea for 600 years and the third largest city in the world, offers many kinds of regional and metropolitan cuisine. The abundance of foodstuffs brought in from every corner of the country has ensured a remarkable variety of recipes, and because of the influence of the royal family and aristocracy, the city boasts elegant table settings and skillful cooking. Much of this old court cuisine has been passed down to the Korean people.

Beef rice soup (seolleongtang), for example, which is made by boiling beef entrails and bones for a whole day, was eaten by the king and the people together after ceremonial prayers for a good harvest. The ceremony was performed at the Sollong Altar in central Seoul, hence the name.

Stewed Beef Ribs (Galbi Jjim, see page 87) is another Seoul specialty, and visitors to the kitchens of traditional Seoul restaurants will often find a huge pot of water, sugar, rice wine, ground pear, radish, carrots, gingko nuts, cinnamon and chestnuts boiling away, ready for preparing the galbi. Grilled Beef Ribs (Galbi Gui, see page 87) are cut off the bone in long, unfolded sections, and then scored and seasoned before being broiled on a grill.

Beef Bulgogi (see page 78) is perhaps one of the best known of Korean foods associated with Seoul. For this dish, a tenderloin or sirloin of beef is sliced thinly, scored lightly for tenderness, then marinated with sugar, rice wine, garlic, sesame oil and soybean sauce, and finally, barbecued over a charcoal fire. It is often accompanied by lettuce leaves, raw whole garlic and spring onions.

Seoul also offers a Spicy Beef Soup (Yukgaejang, see page 60) for Koreans enervated by the humid summer heat. Brisket of beef is deeply broiled and seasoned with hot spices, so much so that people perspire when they eat it, illustrating the Korean philosophy of "fighting heat with heat." When eating this soup, Koreans typically mix a bit of rice into the soup.

OPPOSITE: Seoul is a melting-pot of regional and metropolitan cuisine. Here, a selection of freshly caught seafood is served at Seoul's Sorabol Restaurant, demonstrating the wide variety of seafood available in Korea. BELOW: A 12-cheop (12 side dish) meal, traditionally served only to royalty, now offered by the Sorabol Restaurant at the Shilla Hotel in Seoul. Interestingly, in the past, maps were used to show the traditional placement of each side dish.

On New Year's Day, a sliced rice cake soup (*tteokguk*) is eaten. This is a beef broth in which hardened bars of rice cake are thinly sliced and boiled until almost swollen. More recently, another of Seoul's specialities—*mandu*, or Chinese dumplings—has been added to the broth in place of the rice cakes. Dumplings are one of several Chinese influences on Korean food, epitomizing its eclectic nature.

Kimchi, Chili and Ginseng

"A man can live without a wife, but not without kimchi" is an old Korean saying. "As Korean as kimchi" is another. Even today, it is virtually impossible to find a Korean house, apartment, or monastery without rows of big, black enameled or clay kimchi pots on the porch or balcony, or, in the snowy months, buried in the earth. Some of these vessels are also used to ferment soy sauce and soybean paste which are still made in some households today.

Kimchi can be preserved for a long time. Its hot and spicy taste stimulates the appetite, and it is nutritious, providing vitamins, lactic acid, and minerals otherwise lacking in the winter diet. It is also high in fibre, good for maintaining a healthy bowel. Apparently, it is also believed to prevent cancer.

The introduction of chili into the traditional process of pickling vegetables in the 17th century—a process that dates back a thousand years or more—was an important innovation in Korean food culture. Using chilies in combination with vegetables and fish resulted in a unique method of food preservation and led to the adoption of kimchi as the most important Korean dietary staple.

Red chili and garlic are the mainstays of the basic kimchi formula, which calls for heads of fresh cabbage or other vegetables to be cut open, salted, placed in brine. Later, the vegetables are seasoned with lots of red chili and garlic, and set to ferment. In summer, when fermentation is rapid, kimchi is made fresh every day. In winter, the big kimchi pots are packed in straw and buried in the earth to prevent freezing, then left to ferment for months. Today, most households store their supply of kimchi in a small "kimchi refrigerator", about the size of a small bar refrigerator, at a temperature of 39°F (4°C). There are literally hundreds of kimchi types. There is even a Myongga Kimchi Museum in Seoul that displays them! However, the most common variants are: wrapped kimchi (*bossam kimchi*), comprising seafood such as octopus, shrimp and oyster; white cabbage kimchi (Baek Kimchi), mainly made in the south and containing pickled fish, and sometimes eaten with noodles in winter; Stuffed Cucumber Kimchi (Oisobaegi, see page 28), made with cucumbers stuffed with seasonings; hot radish kimchi (*kkaktugi*), made with Korean white radishes cut into small cubes, seasoned and fermented; "bachelor" radish kimchi (*chonggak kimchi*), made with small salted daikon radishes and anchovies; and Water Kimchi (Nabak Kimchi, see page 28), with slices of daikon radish and pieces of cabbage, mixed with green or red chilies and served chilled.

Besides red chili and garlic, favorite Korean seasonings include spring onion or Korean leek, ginger, sesame oil, sesame seeds, rice wine and soy sauce. The basis of Korean cuisine is in creating a harmony of the five tastes; sweet, sour, salty, hot and bitter. Cooking herbs are used on account of their association with traditional herbal medicine and this is reflected in their daily meals. There are also many fermented soybean pastes and sauces for dipping, called *chang*. Every restaurant and home has its own formula for making *chang*. Based on a fermented mash of soybeans, the three most common varieties are *kanchang* (dark and liquid), *daenchang* (thick and pungent), and *gochuchang* (fiery and hot).

Ginseng (*insam*) is also a staple of the Korean diet; it is also one of Korea's most universally recognized symbols. Due to the root's uncanny resemblance to the anthropoid human form, the Chinese characters that denote ginseng are made up of "man" and "root". Chinese experiments with herbal medicine go back 5,500 years. The earliest medical texts that are known to have survived make ample mention of ginseng, and in medicine, as in many other fields, Korea proved to be China's earliest and best pupil. There is evidence of Chinese medicinal herbs being transplanted into Korea during the third century B.C., and Chinese medical texts have always been widely perused by Korean scholars and healers.

By the mid-17th century, the Dutchman Hendrick Hamel described ginseng as a plant indigenous to Korea. Originally found in remote wild mountains in northern Korea, ginseng is now cultivated throughout the peninsula, especially on Kanghwa Island. The roots are grown in long, neat rows protected from the elements by thatched shelters. After harvesting, they are washed, peeled and dried, then sorted according to age and quality into white ginseng types. Red ginseng, which is regarded by Koreans as the very best, is steamed before being dried in the sun, which is believed to increase its medicinal powers.

Koreans consume an enormous amount of ginseng—as root, pills, capsules, candies, chewing gum, cigarettes, tonics and beauty products. Ginseng Tea (Insam-Cha, see page 108) is a national drink and is available in tea shops everywhere. Many open markets have special ginseng stalls. Even drink stalls, selling coffee, tea and colas, has blenders ready to puree these prized roots with milk and honey into a healthy pick-me-up ginseng shake. Perhaps the most famous ginseng dish is Ginseng Chicken Soup (Samgyetang) which is served in a hotpot. The chicken is stuffed with ginseng, dried red dates, sticky rice and garlic, then stewed. The result is a energizing, tender, flavorsome dish, that is sublimely cooling, believed to replace lost body heat on hot summer days.

RIGHT: Ginseng is cultivated across the Korean Peninsula, and is widely recognized as one of the staples of the Korean diet. This photo shows freshly planted ginseng fields in central Korea, near the Maisan Provincial Park. Straw is placed over the seeds to insulate them from the cold of winter.

Korean Beverages

Drinking has always played an important role in Korean leisure life, especially at the royal court. Many of the oldest ceramics excavated in Korea are drinking cups and liquor vessels, and there are many references to drinking parties in Korean literature and art. Drinking is a national pastime today, and there is no better way for the visitor to delve beneath the veneer of Korean society and get to know Koreans, than by drinking with them in a typical liquor house (*sul-jip*).

Etiquette on drinking occasions includes several traditional customs. When being served by an elder person, the glass is held in both hands. The face is slightly turned away while drinking, and the contents are enjoyed slowly. When the glass is returned to the elder person, it is held in the right hand with the left hand supporting the right elbow gently. The younger persons are expected to keep the glasses of the elder people present full and during pouring, the bottle is held in the right hand and the left hand supports the right elbow.

Such Confucian-style rules sound extremely cumbersome, but it is surprising how relaxed and graceful they can make one feel. Drinking in Korea is a social experience and there is a whole range of Korean liquors, tonics and teas to enjoy. Ginseng liquor (*insam-sul*), for example, is prepared by leaving a whole ginseng root to soak in a bottle of *soju*, a Korean gin made from potatoes, best enjoyed with ginseng chicken. *Soju* leaves a bad hangover if taken in excess and the best remedy is a ginseng tonic. A more acceptable version is *makgeolli*, a milky white brew that is fermented from rice and said to be highly nutritious. There are many traditional *makgeolli* drinking establishments in Seoul and the provincial cities. These are well worth a visit for their old-fashioned wooden decor, the snacks (*anju*) they serve, and their air of conviviality. *Popchu*, a high-grade rice wine similar to Japanese sake and usually served hot, is a specialty of Konju, in central Korea. Other alcoholic beverages such as beer has also become increasingly popular in Korea, especially the bottled variety, while draught beer can be found in the many beer halls (*tong-dalkjip*) specializing in broiled chicken.

Koreans never drink without *anju*. These snacks absorb the alcohol and create a thirst. Favorite *anju* are soybean curd; raw crab legs marinated in red chili sauce; sliced raw fish; fish roe in garlic sauce; blanched spinach dressed with sesame oil and seeds, dried anchovies sautéed with red chilies; broiled fish sprinkled with sesame seeds; green garlic pickled in soy sauce; sautéed oysters, beef and bean curd patties spiced with ginger; mung bean pancake laced with shrimp; and ground beef patties with garlic and sesame seeds.

A variety of delicious teas are usually served with traditional Korean cuisine, but not all are from the tea plant. Koreans prefer teas brewed from grains, dried fruits and ginseng. Popular teas today include barley tea (*bori-cha*)—the national beverage which is served free of charge at every restaurant and tearoom in the country, and which is often served cold in homes and drunk at nearly every meal, other teas include quince tea (*mogwa-cha*), walnut tea (*hodo-cha*), ginseng tea (*insam-cha*), citron tea (*yuja-cha*), red date tea (*daechu-cha*) and roasted corn tea (*oksusu-cha*).

Green tea (*nok-cha*) was the first tea introduced to Korea, arriving during the reign of Queen Seondeok (A.D. 632–647) of the Silla Kingdom (57 B.C.–A.D. 935). Annual green tea festivals are still held in green tea plantations in Boseonggun, Gyeongsangnamdo, Jeollanamdo and Hadonggun. Teahouses in Korea offer a wide variety of teas in elegant antique interiors against a backdrop of traditional Korean music. Free tea tastings are sometimes also conducted. Sweet desserts to be served with tea, particularly on festive occasions, include deep-fried cereals (*yugwa*); roots or fruit stewed in honey or sugar syrup (*jeongwa*); honey-nut nougat; and steamed rice and nuts in sesame oil and honey (*dasik*).

LEFT: Over 1,000 shops and stalls at Seoul's Gyeongdong Herbal Market sell traditional herbs, Korean ginseng and a variety of teas. BELOW: Tea served in the traditional manner at the Yeong Bin Gwan Guest House in the Shilla Hotel, Seoul.

Eating and Cooking in Korea
Preparing and enjoying an authentic Korean meal.

In traditional Korean kitchens, cooks prepared dishes over a wood fire and cooking was very labor intensive. But in modern times, the wood fire has since been replaced by modern conveniences such as the gas and electric stove, making cooking both convenient and easy. Apart from a couple of unusual cooking or serving instruments, most of the important utensils are very common. A **heavy skillet** is recommended, as is a **wok** for stir-frying, and some sturdy **saucepans** and large **casserole dishes** are essential.

Koreans, like most Asians, eat a lot of rice—though in ancient times they ate millet. Koreans are fond of adding other grains to their rice, like millet or black soybeans. Korean rice is short-grain, similar to the rice favored by the Japanese. To cook rice on a regular basis, an **electric rice cooker** is a must as it is easy to use and produces perfectly fluffy rice without fuss. Rice that has been rinsed clean in a few changes of water is simply placed inside the rice cooker with water, switched on and left to cook automatically. Most electric rice cookers also have a "keep warm" function to keep the rice steaming hot, leaving you with plenty of time to prepare other dishes.

The Korean barbecue, well known throughout the world, is a popular way of cooking beef in restaurants and street stalls. At home, families usually use a **tabletop grill** on which to cook *bulgogi* and *galbi* ribs. The grill is dome-shaped, made of brass or stainless steel, with protruding perforated holes and a skirting around the base to collect drippings from the seared meat. Some upmarket restaurants are equipped with vacuum exhaust pipes directly next to the griddle to suck up the smoke.

Nothing satisfies like a steaming hotpot of soup or stew in winter. A must-have in a Korean household is the **hotpot** (ttukbaegi), a round clay casserole pot with a cover, used for cooking soups and stews. This hotpot is placed directly on the fire or an electric hotplate and then trans ferred to the table. It serves to keep

the food hot during the meal.

Many families also own a specially designed metal pot used in preparing hotpot meals. This unusual vessel, which is also called a **firekettle**, **chafing** or **steamboat pot**, has a central chimney that is surrounded by a moat. Hot coals are inserted into the chimney and a hot broth is poured into the moat and kept simmering by the heat of the coals.

Diners then select food items from the hot broth—a delicious and very social way of dining! These days, the charcoal-fueled steam hotpots have been replaced by electrical ones with temperature control. Some hotpots can simply sit on a portable gas or electric stove. These are available from Asian food stores. Otherwise, an easy alternative is to use an **electric wok** or deep electric pan that can be placed in the middle of the dining table, and that is also large enough to hold broth as well as ingredients like meat and vegetables.

Visitors to the Korean kitchen will no doubt notice an array of earthenware crocks or storage jars. These are not for display but are used, even today, to store and ferment Korean foods such as *ganjang* (soy sauce), *gochujang* (Korean chili bean paste), *deonjang* (fermented soybean paste), and kimchi. The pots keep their contents from going bad and keep kimchi fresh for a long time.

The *jangdokdae* is the place where Koreans place the pots used to store fermented food. It is usually located in the backyard near the kitchen in a high area with plenty of sunshine and good ventilation. It is traditional for soybean pastes and sauces to be made in the spring, while the process of kimchi making usually begins in the fall.

Korean Dining Etiquette
Korean table settings are classified as 3-*cheop*, 5-*cheop*, 7-*cheop*, 9-*cheop* or 12-*cheop*, according to the number

OPPOSITE: The traditional Korean kitchen featured a fire stove, which is increasingly rare today. TOP: A kimchi urn, still in use today to store kimchi. LEFT: A clay urn for fermented foods such as soy sauce or soybean paste; a steamer, usually covered with a damp cloth; a stoneware pot usually placed directly over heat keeps soups and stews hot during the meal. This pot can also be made of clay or cast iron.

of side dishes (*cheop*) served at a meal. For an everyday Korean meal, the average family takes about four or five side dishes, along with rice—traditionally the center of all table arrangements—plus soup and kimchi. The main meals include breakfast, which is the most fortifying meal of the day, a lighter lunch (called *jeomsin*, which means "to lighten the heart"), and a not-too-heavy dinner.

The basic *bansang* formal (table) setting includes seven side dishes with boiled rice, soup, three seasoning sauces—such as red chili bean paste, kimchi and hot radish kimchi—and two heavier soups, such as a hot pollack or rib stew. These soups are considered an accompaniment to the meal and not a starter. Except for the individual bowl of rice and soup, the dishes are shared.

Younger diners are expected to wait for their elders before starting a meal. When the elder diners hold up their spoon, this is a signal to the rest of the diners that they may begin to eat. Rice, soups and stews are eaten with a spoon, and the rather dry side dishes are eaten with metal chopsticks. The spoon and chopsticks are not used at the same time—when chopsticks are being used, the spoon is left on the table. Bowls and plates are also not raised from the table.

It may be confusing to know where to start when faced with the numerous side dishes and main courses, but usually the soups are tasted first, before eating some rice and starting on the remaining dishes. As the younger diners are expected to stay at the dining table until the elder diners finish, try to pace yourself with the other diners. A traditional Korean meal is served at a low table, with diners seated on cushions on an *ondol* floor—a Korean heating system where hot water is run through pipes laid under the floor, providing ample heating in the winter months.

The ceremonial aspect of Korean dining has been greatly influenced by Confucianism and the royal court. There are abundant archives of royal dishes in Korea and some of them can still be experienced in their entirety. For example, Gujeolpan (Royal Spring Roll Platter, see page 36) is served in an octagonal lacquered platter with nine compartments. Delicate pancakes are placed in the center, surrounded by eight other treasures to be carefully wrapped inside the pancakes. Another royal delicacy is Shinseolo (see page 73) , which translates as "the food of hermits in fairyland" and which comes in a brass pot with a chimney, rather like a Mongolian hotpot. The hotpot is served with a variety of ingredients, such as fish, vegetables, chestnuts, gingko nuts and little, delicate meatballs simmered in broth. The cuisine of the royal court is the basis for an elaborate à la carte presentation of foods called *teukbyeol yori* or "specialties", which range from appetizers to rice cakes and cookies.

Many festivals in Korea are based on the lunar calendar, and the food prepared for these festivals is symbolic and most appropriate to the season. The New Year's Day Table, following a Confucian ceremony honoring one's ancestors, includes sweet rice, three-colored vegetables and *gujeolpan*.

The first full moon of the year is celebrated with dried vegetables from the previous year, and five kinds of grains—plain rice, glutinous rice, millet, corn and red beans—in a special dish. Wine is also drunk, believed to prevent deafness.

Chuseok, or Thanksgiving for the newly harvested rice, is marked by rice cakes in a half-moon shape and by five grains, both of which are a mark of respect to ancestors. On Ancestor's Memorial Day, food is presented at the grave site and eaten there, while on Buddha's Birthday, mountain vegetables are the main dish of the day. Other culinary festivities include preparing evil-dispelling pounded rice cakes on January 1st, and glutinous rice cakes with angelika petals on the Buddhist festival of hair washing. At Confucian and shamanist ceremonies, an offering is made of a pig's head stuffed with money.

A Bride's Gift Table comprises stuffed dried red dates, broiled beef patties, chestnuts, a nine-sectioned dish, and wine and chicken in tasseled handkerchiefs, while a 61st Birthday Table is a large feast that is served because the lunar calendar has reached its span of 60 years and is set to begin again. The Korean people thus celebrate the passing of each season with a full culinary calendar, the fruit of their Buddhist Confucian background and rich agricultural heritage.

OPPOSITE: Kimchi and other side dishes make up a "5-side dish" meal. Kimchi is Korea's "national dish" and passion—literally hundreds of different kinds of kimchi are made, and a normal meal will feature at least five or six different variants. ABOVE: A restaurant patron enjoying a typical Korean meal of kimchi and a wide variety of side dishes. BELOW: An octagonal lacquered platter with nine compartments, traditionally used for serving *gujeolpan* to royalty. An elegant appetizer eaten by rolling small amounts of savory fillings in tiny pancakes and dipped in Lemon Mustard Sauce. Soft, delicate pancakes lie in the center of the tray, surrounded by sumptuous fillings of beef and vegetables.

Authentic Korean Ingredients

Bamboo shoots are available pre-cooked—whole or sliced—in vacuum packs in well-stocked supermarkets. These precooked shoots are crunchy, with a savory sweetness, and are much easier to use than fresh shoots, which need to be boiled for about 2 hours. Canned bamboo shoots are also common, but not as tasty, and should be drained, rinsed and scalded in hot water before use. Store unused shoots in the refrigerator, immersed in water. If you change the water daily, bamboo shoots keep for up to 10 days.

Bean sprouts grown from mung beans are the common variety available in most supermarkets. Soybean sprouts, a larger variety, are also available in many stores. Soybean sprouts take a little longer to cook, have a nutty flavor, and are excellent blanched or stir-fried with chives and fish sauce or sesame oil as a side dish. Always try to purchase sprouts fresh as they lose their crisp texture quite quickly. They will keep in the refrigerator, immersed in water, for a few days.

Bracken, also known as fiddlehead fern or fernbrake, are the edible young sprouts of the fern plant. Bracken are about 7 in (18 cm) long, with rounded violin-like heads curled in tight circles. Only the top portion of the sprouts and the tender leaves are edible. Rinse fresh bracken, thoroughly to remove any dirt, rub them between your palms to remove any hair, then discard the tough stalks. Dried bracken should be rinsed and soaked overnight (see recipe on page 60). Look for fresh or dried bracken in Korean specialty stores, or substitute with baby asparagus, which has a similar woody texture and flavor.

Chili peppers called for in this book are finger-length Asian chilies with medium heat. **Dried chili flakes** are made by coarsely crushing sundried red chilies. **Korean ground red pepper** is made by deseeding dried red chilies, then grinding them to a powder, and the color is darker and the flavor richer than other ground peppers. Korean ground red pepper develops a creamy consistency when cooked with other ingredients, and is not as hot as the dark red color might indicate. Substitute with any other ground red pepper, but you may need to reduce the quantity if you are using a particularly hot variety. Korean **dried chili strips** are dried, thinly sliced and roasted. They are mild and crispy, ideal as a garnish. Although Korean dried chilies and ground red pepper are difficult to find, it is worth seeking them out.

Corn syrup is available bottled and is clear or light gold in color. If a small quantity is called for, it is often easier to make your own sugar syrup by boiling 2 tablespoons of sugar in 4 tablespoons water until the liquid thickens. **Malt syrup**, which has a light molasses flavor, also makes a good substitute.

Chinese cabbage, also known as Napa cabbage, has tightly packed white stems and pale green leaves. It has a mild, delicate taste and is a good source of minerals such as calcium, potassium and iron. Chinese cabbage is the basic ingredient in kimchi and is also commonly eaten in many soups.

Chinese chives, also known as garlic chives, have a garlicky flavor and aroma. Unlike Western chives, which have rounded stems, Chinese chives resemble flat spring onions and are sold in bunches in the produce section of Asian food stores. When buying, look for fresh stems—the ends should snap off easily.

Chrysanthemum greens are the tender edible leaves of the giant chrysanthemum plant. The serrated leaves have a slightly bitter, grassy flavor. They are often used as a garnish and a flavoring in Korean soups. A more commonly available variety is garland Chrysanthemum, also known by its Chinese name *tung ho*, are sold in bunches often with the roots attached. Store refrigerated and wrapped in paper. Substitute with Chinese celery leaves or watercress.

Daikon radishes are large and juicy root vegetables also known as white radishes or giant radishes. The Korean daikon (*mu*) is large and round. The recipes in this book call for sections of large Japanese daikons which are about 3 in (8 cm) in diameter. These radishes can grow to a length of 15 in (40 cm) or more. They are sold in sections in supermarkets. Choose firm and heavy daikons without any bruises on them. Scrub or peel the skin before you grate or slice the flesh.

Dried chestnuts are sweeter than fresh roasted chestnuts. They are sold in small cellophane packets and need to be rehydrated by soaking them in water for 30 to 40 minutes before use.

Dried kelp (*konbu*) is a brown seaweed sold in small, folded sheets. Wipe the salt off the surface with a damp cloth before use. Do not rinse or wash the kelp as it will lose its flavor. When cooked, the kelp expands into smooth, green sheets and these are used in Korean dishes to add flavoring and color to soup stocks. The kelp should be discarded before serving the dish.

Dried red dates are also known as Chinese dates or jujubes. They are native to the Mediterranean as well as China, and are used in both sweet and savory dishes as a flavoring. Look for bright, deep red dates.

Dried pollack, a type of cod, is sold whole and deboned, or in shaved strips. A delicacy in Korea, this dried fish is not salted. It is available from Korean specialty stores. If using salt cod or other types of dried salted fish, slice and then soak it overnight and squeeze dry before use to remove as much of the salt as possible.

Fermented Korean bean paste is a thick, smooth paste made from fermented soybeans and grains similar to Japanese miso, sugar and salt. It is one of the most important seasonings in the Korean kitchen. There are two main varieties—**soybean paste** (*deonjang*) and **chili bean paste** (*gochujang*). Soybean paste (*deonjang*) is made from soybeans, barley, sugar and salt, is brown in color and has a salty-sweet taste. Chili bean paste (*gochujang*) is dark red in color and is made of soy, malt liquid and ground red pepper, and has a spicy taste. Both are available from Korean specialty stores and well-stocked supermarkets. *Doenjang* may be substituted with miso paste or other fermented soybean pastes with a bit of added sugar. Substitute *gochujang* with other chili bean pastes or make your own by mixing 2 tablespoons miso paste (or mashed fermented soybean), 1 teaspoon corn, malt or sugar syrup and $^1/_2$–1 teaspoon ground red pepper.

Fermented shrimp are tiny shrimp that have been salted and left to ferment for 3 to 4 months. They have a pungent smell and are a popular ingredient in Korean cooking. They are used to make kimchi, while the juice is often used to flavor other Korean dishes. Look for plastic packets of fermented shrimp in the refrigerated section of Asian food stores.

Fish sauce in Korea is less salty and fishy than the Thai variety. If you are using Thai fish sauce, reduce the quantity called for in the recipe by approximately one quarter.

Gingko nuts have a hard shell and are spherical in shape. The Korean variety is small, green and tender on the inside, unlike the common Chinese variety. Shelled white nuts are sold in Asian food stores in two forms—either refrigerated in plastic packets or canned. If using whole unshelled gingko nuts, boil them in water for about 7 minutes, drain and crack open to remove the hard shells. Soak the nuts in water to loosen the skins around them.

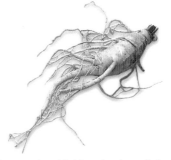

Ginseng is a highly prized medicinal root believed to have rejuvenating properties. It is widely cultivated in Korea and used extensively in Korean cooking. As aged ginseng root is very expensive, substitute cheaper, vacuum-packed white ginseng (similar in taste to parsnips). Another alternative is to use dried ginseng root shavings and strings, available from Asian food stores and apothecaries.

Authentic Korean Recipes

Planning a Korean meal

Korean meals are usually shared family-style; and many small plates containing side dishes of kimchi, *namul* (seasoned vegetables) and sauces are usually placed in the center of the dining table alongside the main dishes for everyone to help themselves. A fancy meal for 4 to 6 people might start with an appetizer like Grilled Beef and Mushroom Skewers or Fresh Seafood Pancakes. Main dishes could include a balance of meat, poultry, seafood and vegetable dishes, such as Transparent Noodles with Beef and Vegetables, Beef Bulgogi or Fried Kimchi Rice with Beef. Numerous side dishes can include a healthy vegetable dish, like Seasoned Korean Vegetables or Classic Chinese Cabbage Kimchi, or a hearty Braised Garlic Soy Beef dish. You can also serve individual bowls of rice and a soup such as Pollack Soup with Daikon or Vegetables and Tofu Simmered in Bean Paste. Dessert is not usually part of a Korean meal, but fresh fruit or a refreshing light dessert, like Persimmon Sherbet, is an excellent way to complete a meal. As a general guide, the recipes in this book will serve 4–6 people for a meal consisting of rice, soup, one or two side dishes, as well as two to three main dishes.

Korean seasonings and Ingredients

Korean seasonings are simple—a delicate balance of typical Asian ingredients such as dried red chilies, garlic, good quality soy, and sesame oil—combined with fresh produce to achieve a perfect blend of spicy, sweet, sour and salty flavors. Other essential seasonings are sesame seeds, soybean paste (*deonjang*) and chili bean paste (*gochujang*). Once you have these basics on your kitchen shelf, you're well on your way to preparing an authentic Korean meal. Traditional Korean households make their own soybean paste and chili bean paste at home, but prepared versions are readily available at Korean specialty stores and Asian food stores these days. Koreans are generous in their use of ground red pepper; the Korean variety is a dark red color, but don't worry, the taste is not as spicy as the color may suggest as sundried chilies are used. Sesame oil and sesame seeds are important in Korean cooking for flavor as well as aroma. Vegetables are blanched and lightly seasoned with sesame oil or sesame seeds, and soups receive a sprinkling of sesame oil so that a delightful fragrance wafts gently from the serving dish straight to the table.

Fresh ingredients used in Korean cuisine—like leeks, spring onions, daikon radishes and tofu, can be easily found in almost any supermarket. It is worthwhile also making a trip to a Korean specialty store to buy Korean dried chili peppers, ground red pepper, soy sauce and sesame oil, and dried goods such as dried pollack, whitebait and bracken. Try to locate a Korean or Japanese supermarket for dry goods, or refer to the list of mail order/online sources on page 112 for ingredients that are difficult to find.

Sesame Paste Dip

$^1/_2$ cup (75 g) sesame seeds
2 tablespoons soy sauce
2 tablespoons rice vinegar
1 tablespoon sugar

1 Heat a nonstick skillet over low to medium heat and dry-roast the sesame seeds, stirring continuously for 1 to 2 minutes until the seeds turn golden brown. Allow to cool, then blend to a paste with the soy sauce, rice vinegar and sugar in a blender or food processor. This sauce is a deliciously classic accompaniment to almost any Korean dish.

Yields $^1/_2$ cup (125 ml)
Preparation time: 5 mins
Cooking time: 5 mins

Seafood Glazing Sauce

2 cloves garlic, minced
1 teaspoon grated ginger
$^1/_2$ cup (125 ml) beef or chicken stock
$1^1/_2$ tablespoons soy sauce
$1^1/_2$ tablespoons sugar
1 tablespoon rice wine or sake
1 teaspoon sesame oil
1–2 teaspoons ground red pepper

1 Place all the ingredients in a small saucepan and bring to a boil. Reduce the heat and simmer for about 10 minutes, or until the sauce has reduced by half. Use this glazing sauce to brush over fresh seafood before grilling.

Yields $^1/_2$ cup (125 ml)
Preparation time: 5 mins
Cooking time: 10 mins

Classic Chinese Cabbage Kimchi

Kimchi—a fermented vegetable condiment—is served with every Korean meal. It is very high in Vitamin B, minerals and lactic acid, and can be quite addictive. Mature, sour kimchi is the base for many Korean soups and stir-fries. This classic kimchi is made with Chinese cabbage, chives, daikon radish and leek, and is seasoned with chili, garlic and ginger. For a sour kimchi, cover and store in a cool place for 1–2 days to ferment, then keep refrigerated for up to 3 months. Kimchi can also be eaten fresh (see note below).

1 large Chinese or Napa cabbage (about 3 lbs/$1^1/_2$ kg)
$^3/_4$ cup (210 g) sea salt, coarse salt or pickling salt
8 cups (2 liters) water

Kimchi Spice Mixture
4 tablespoons glutinous rice flour
$1^1/_2$ cups (375 ml) water
3 tablespoons crushed garlic
$^1/_2$ in (2 cm) ginger, peeled and crushed
4 tablespoons fish sauce
  or 1 tablespoon fermented shrimp plus 2 tablespoons fish sauce
8–10 tablespoons ground red pepper
$^1/_2$ tablespoon sugar
8 oz (250 g) daikon radish (about 4 in/10 cm), sliced into 2 in (5 cm) strips
$1^1/_2$ cups (90 g) Chinese chives, sliced into 2 in (5 cm) lengths
$^1/_2$ leek, thinly sliced diagonally

1 Rinse the cabbage, remove two outer leaves and set aside. Halve the rest of the cabbage lengthwise. Rub $^1/_4$ cup of the sea salt between all the leaves and place the cabbage in a large plastic tub or container. Add the remaining salt and the water. Place a big plate on top the cabbage to weigh it down and keep the cabbage immersed in the brine. Soak for 4 to 6 hours or more, until the stems soften and bend without breaking.
2 To make the Kimchi Spice Mixture, first make a glutinous rice flour paste by heating the flour and the water in a small saucepan. Stir constantly until it thickens, about 4 minutes, then set aside to cool. Once it has cooled, combine with the garlic, ginger, fish sauce, red pepper and sugar in a large bowl and mix well. Add the daikon, chives and leek, mix gently and set aside.
3 After the cabbage has finished soaking, rinse the leaves thoroughly under running water. Fill a tub or container with fresh water and shake the two halves of the cabbage backwards and forwards vigorously to remove the salt. Squeeze the cabbage firmly to remove excess water and set aside to drain.
4 Rub the Kimchi Spice Mixture all over the cabbage and in between all the leaves. Press the leaves together and place into a large airtight container. Top with the reserved outer leaves and cover. Leave the kimchi to stand unrefrigerated overnight, then refrigerate.

Note: To make **fresh kimchi** that can be eaten immediately, first cut the cabbage into bite-sized pieces, then sprinkle the sea salt and soak in the water for 2 hours and continue with the recipe. Never use a reactive metal to store kimchi; use porcelain, stainless steel or sturdy plastic.

Makes 3 lbs ($1^1/_2$ kg)   Preparation time: 30 mins + 6 hours soaking + overnight refrigerating time   Cooking time: 5 mins

Water Kimchi   Nabak Kimchi

Natural and lightly fermented, Water Kimchi is slightly tangy and sweet to taste. This cool and refreshing soup—with crunchy, light vegetables and fruits—is best served chilled.

2$^1/_2$ teaspoons ground red pepper
1 teaspoon crushed garlic
$^1/_2$ teaspoon grated ginger
4 teaspoons salt
2 teaspoons sugar
8 cups (2 liters) water
10 oz (300 g) Chinese cabbage, cut
   into squares
2 apples or 1 large nashi pear,
   peeled, cored and sliced
1 Japanese cucumber, halved, then
   sliced lengthwise into strips
$^1/_2$ carrot, halved, then sliced lengthwise into strips
7 oz (200 g) daikon radish (about
   3 in/8 cm), sliced
2 spring onions, cut into lengths
2 green chilies, sliced (optional)

1 Place the red pepper, garlic, ginger, salt and sugar in a large mixing bowl and add the water. Stir to mix well and strain the mixture using a very fine sieve, mashing the red pepper, garlic and ginger through the sieve.
2 Add the cabbage, apples, cucumber, carrot, daikon, spring onions and green chilies, if using, to the strained mixture. Mix thoroughly, then place in an airtight jar or container and refrigerate overnight. The Water Kimchi keeps for 8 days in the refrigerator.

Makes 12 cups (3 liters)   Preparation time: 30 mins + overnight refrigerating time

Stuffed Cucumber Kimchi   Oisobaegi

10 Japanese cucumbers
   (about 1$^1/_2$ lbs/750 g)
3 tablespoons sea salt

Stuffing
10 stalks Chinese chives, rinsed,
   drained and cut into lengths
4 cloves garlic, crushed
$^3/_4$ tablespoon minced ginger
4 tablespoons ground red pepper
$^1/_2$ tablespoon brown sugar
2 tablespoons fish sauce

Serves 4   Preparation time: 60 mins

1 Combine all the Stuffing ingredients and set aside.
2 Rub 1 tablespoon of the sea salt over the cucumbers, then rinse thoroughly. Cut the cucumbers into short sections, about 2 in (5 cm) in length.
3 Cut through the center of each cucumber lengthwise, stopping three-quarters of the way down. Make another lengthwise slit at a right angle to the cut made earlier, forming a cross at the top of each cucumber.
4 Toss the cucumbers gently with the remaining sea salt, then leave to sit for 20 minutes (If using baby Asian cucumbers, they should sit for 40 minutes). Wash the salt from the cucumbers and drain thoroughly. Squeeze gently to remove any excess water.
5 Push the Stuffing into the slits in the cucumber sections and pack in tight rows in an airtight container. The kimchi may be eaten immediately or stored in the refrigerator for up to 8 days. For a more sour kimchi, leave it aside for 4 hours, then store in the refrigerator for 8 days.

Daikon Radish Kimchi

3 lbs (1$^1/_2$ kg) daikon radish, peeled
   and cut into large chunks
3 tablespoons sea salt
1 portion Kimchi Spice Mixture
   (page 27)

Serves 4–6   Preparation time: 20 mins

1 Sprinkle the daikon with the sea salt and leave to sit for 20 minutes.
2 Wash and rinse the daikon thoroughly to remove all the salt.
3 Rub the Kimchi Spice Mixture over the daikon and place in an airtight container. Cover the container, leave to stand overnight, then refrigerate. This is an excellent accompaniment to noodle dishes like Chilled Summer Noodles with Beef and Vegetables (page 53).

Seasoned Korean Vegetables   Namul

Side dishes of blanched vegetables, delicately seasoned and prepared with minimum oil, are almost invariably served as part of a main Korean meal. All kinds of vegetables like spinach greens, mushroom, eggplant, daikon radish, cucumber and fresh bean sprouts can all be prepared in this fashion.

10 oz (300 g) spinach, washed and drained
8 oz (250 g) bamboo shoots, slivered
1 tablespoon sesame oil
2 teaspoons toasted sesame seeds, crushed
1 teaspoon salt
20 fresh shiitake mushrooms (about 5 oz/150 g), stems discarded
  and caps sliced
$1/_3$ cup (80 ml) water
$1^1/_2$ tablespoons soy sauce
2 tablespoons rice wine or sake
1 teaspoon sugar
Toasted sesame seeds, to garnish

1 Cover the bottom of a large saucepan or pot with water and bring to a boil. Blanch the spinach. Drain and roughly chop the spinach and squeeze out any excess liquid. Combine the spinach with 1 teaspoon of the sesame oil, 1 teaspoon of the crushed sesame seeds and a $1/_2$ teaspoon of the salt. Arrange the spinach neatly on a serving dish. Repeat with the bamboo shoots and arrange them neatly beside the spinach.
2 Place the mushrooms in a small saucepan and add the water, the remaining sesame oil, soy sauce, rice wine and sugar. Bring to a boil, cover, and simmer for 5 minutes, or until the mushrooms are cooked.
3 Transfer the mushrooms to the serving dish and arrange decoratively beside the other vegetables. Sprinkle the toasted sesame seeds and serve warm or at room temperature.

Note: If fresh shiitake mushrooms are not available, substitute 15 dried black Chinese mushrooms. Soak for 30 minutes before use.

Serves 4   Preparation time: 20 mins   Cooking time: 8 mins

Raw Korean Beef Tartare Salad Yukhoe

An appetizer that really opens the taste buds—this simple and satisfying salad of thin, raw slices of beef and crunchy nashi pear is coated in a sweet and spicy sesame-garlic sauce. It is wrapped in lettuce leaves and dipped in egg yolk, and simply popped into the mouth. Also a popular pub snack, it is often served with beaten egg yolk on the side.

7 oz (200 g) beef fillet, sliced into thin strips
4–6 lettuce leaves, washed and drained
$1/2$ tablespoon pine nuts, finely ground
1–2 cloves garlic, very thinly sliced
$1/2$ large nashi pear (about $1^3/_4$ cups/300 g), peeled and finely diced
1 teaspoon lime or lemon juice
Pine nuts, to garnish
1 egg yolk, to serve (optional)

Sauce
1 tablespoon soy sauce
2 teaspoons sugar
1 teaspoon crushed garlic
1 teaspoon sesame oil
1 teaspoon toasted sesame seeds, coarsely crushed
1–2 teaspoons ground red pepper (optional)
Freshly ground black pepper

1 Wrap the beef in plastic wrap and chill in the freezer for 30 minutes. Remove the plastic wrap and slice the beef very thinly, and then into strips.
2 Mix all the Sauce ingredients together, then combine with the beef slices, tossing to mix well.
3 Line a plate with the lettuce leaves and place the marinated beef in the center of the plate. Scatter the plate with the pine nuts and garlic.
4 Toss the pear with the lime juice and arrange around the beef. Garnish with the pine nuts and serve the egg yolk (if using) in small dipping bowls.

Note: If it's difficult to find nashi pear, simply substitute with a crunchy apple or jicama. Use sashimi instead of beef, if desired.

Serves 4   Preparation time: 30 mins

Grilled Beef and Mushroom Skewers   Songi Sanjeok

10 oz (300 g) oyster or beefsteak
   mushrooms
4 oz (125 g) beef
8 spring onions, white part only
Short bamboo skewers

Sauce
2 tablespoons soy sauce
1 teaspoon brown sugar
1 clove garlic, crushed
1 teaspoon minced spring onion
1 teaspoon sesame seeds
$1/_2$ teaspoon sesame oil
1 tablespoon rice wine or sake
$1/_4$ teaspoon salt (optional)
Pinch of ground red pepper (optional)

1 Combine all the Sauce ingredients, mix thoroughly and set aside.
2 Cut the mushrooms, beef and spring onions into strips that are approximately the same in length and thickness. Thread pieces of mushrooms, beef and spring onions through the skewer. Repeat until all the ingredients are used up.
3 Brush the skewered ingredients with the Sauce and cook under a hot grill, or sear in a hot, nonstick skillet and cook for 2 to 3 minutes on each side until the beef and mushrooms are cooked. Serve warm.

Makes 8 skewers   Preparation time: 10 mins   Cooking time: 5 mins

Pan-fried Mushrooms   Songi Gui

5 fresh pine, shiitake, beefsteak
   or porcini mushrooms
$1/_4$ teaspoon salt
1 tablespoon vegetable oil
1 teaspoon sesame oil

1 Dab the mushrooms with paper towels to remove any moisture, then slice them into 4 or 5 pieces. Sprinkle the salt over the mushroom pieces.
2 Heat the vegetable oil in a skillet over medium heat and stir-fry the mushrooms for 3 to 4 minutes, or until the mushrooms are cooked. Drizzle the sesame oil and serve warm.

Serves 4   Preparation time: 5 mins   Cooking time: 5 mins

Royal Spring Roll Platter   Gujeolpan

Each person creates his or her own rolled pancakes at the table and dips it in the sauce.

1 large egg, lightly beaten
1 small Japanese cucumber, sliced into thin shreds
1 small carrot, sliced into thin shreds
1 green bell pepper, sliced into thin shreds
$1/2$ cup (50 g) slivered bamboo shoots, blanched in boiling water, then drained
1 teaspoon salt
1 teaspoon sesame oil
8 spring onions, cut into lengths
1canned abalone or smoked oyster, sliced into thin shreds (optional)
1 tablespoon crushed pine nuts, to garnish

Mushroom Filling
8 dried black Chinese mushrooms, soaked in $1/2$ cup (125 ml) hot water for 30 minutes, stems discarded and caps shredded; soaking liquid reserved
$1^1/2$ teaspoons soy sauce
$3/4$ teaspoon sugar
$1/4$ teaspoon sesame oil

Beef Filling
8 oz (250 g) beef fillet, sliced into very fine strips
2 teaspoons soy sauce
$1/2$ teaspoon crushed garlic
$1/2$ teaspoon sugar
1 teaspoon sesame oil
2 teaspoons vegetable oil

Pancakes
2 cups (250 g) flour, sifted
$1/2$ teaspoon salt
2 eggs, lightly beaten
$2^1/4$ cups (560 ml) water
2 teaspoons vegetable oil

1 Place all the Mushroom Filling ingredients in a small saucepan. Cover with water and simmer for 20 minutes. Drain and set aside.
2 To prepare the Beef Filling, combine the beef with the soy sauce, garlic, sugar and sesame oil. Heat the vegetable oil in a wok, add the seasoned beef and stir-fry over high heat for 5 minutes. Remove and set aside.
3 To make the Pancakes, place the flour and salt in a bowl, then add the eggs and mix well. Add the water gradually, mixing thoroughly to form a smooth batter. If desired, add a few drops of food coloring. Heat the oil in a large skillet, then pour in 2 tablespoons of the batter to make a thin Pancake. Repeat until all the batter is used up and set the Pancakes aside.
4 Make a very thin omelet with the beaten egg, then slice it into very thin shreds. Form the sliced eggs into a small mound and place it on a large platter. Toss the cucumber with a $1/4$ teaspoon salt and a $1/4$ teaspoon sesame oil. Repeat with the carrot, bell pepper and bamboo shoots, and place them next to the other fillings.
5 Place all the fillings for the spring rolls in separate mounds on a large serving platter and garnish with the pine nuts. Serve with Mustard and Lemon Sauce (page 90) and soy sauce.

Serves 4   Preparation time: 50 mins   Cooking time: 50 mins

Soft Tofu with Spicy Sesame Sauce
Yangnyeumjang Sundubu

A deliciously simple way of serving tofu. Chilled tofu is drizzled with a little spicy, sesame-flavored sauce and garnished generously with thin strips of dried chili. A light side dish, perfect on a hot summer night.

1 lb (500 g) silken or soft tofu, chilled and cut into 4 pieces or left whole
1 spring onion, minced, to garnish
$^1/_2$ red chili, deseeded and minced
  or dried red chili strips or chili flakes, to garnish (optional)

Spicy Sesame Sauce
1 tablespoon soy sauce
1 teaspoon sesame oil
1 clove garlic, finely minced
$^1/_2$ red chili, finely minced (optional)
1 teaspoon ground red pepper
1 teaspoon water
2 teaspoons toasted sesame seeds, crushed
2 spring onions, minced

1 To make the sauce, combine all the ingredients, mix well and set aside.
2 Place the 4 pieces of tofu into individual serving bowls, or into one large serving bowl if using a whole piece of tofu. Drizzle the Spicy Sesame Sauce over the tofu and garnish with the spring onion and chili. Serve as an appetizer or as a side dish with steaming hot rice.

Note: If silken tofu is not available, substitute with a chilled block of regular tofu sliced into bite-sized pieces and coat well with the sauce.

Serves 4   Preparation time: 10 mins

Braised Garlic Soy Beef Sogogi Jangchorim

This simple and delicious recipe requires little preparation although it does take some time to cook. While waiting for the meat to cook, you can prepare the rice and a vegetable dish or two to accompany the beef, along with a side dish of kimchi.

1 medium onion, quartered
3 bulbs of garlic, peeled
2 cups (500 ml) water
$1/2$ cup (125 ml) soy sauce
2 teaspoons sugar
6 hard-boiled quail eggs or 2 hard-boiled eggs, to serve

Boiled Beef and Stock
2 lbs (1 kg) boneless skirt steak, or other stewing beef parts like chuck, shin, shank or brisket
8 cups (2 liters) water

1 Place the beef in a pot with the water, bring to a boil and simmer for 10 minutes. Skim off all the unwanted residue that rises to the top. Cover, reduce the heat and simmer very gently for $1^1/_2$ hours until the meat is just tender. Remove the beef. Strain the stock and set aside, reserving it for other dishes.
2 Shred the meat and return it to the pot. Add the remaining ingredients, except the quail eggs and bring to a boil. Cover, then reduce the heat and simmer over low heat for 30 to 45 minutes, stirring from time to time until the beef is very tender. Serve with the quail eggs and freshly steamed rice.

Note: If desired, peel the hard-boiled quail eggs and add to the soup in the last 5 minutes of simmering. The beef stock, prepared above, can be kept frozen for 3 months.

Serves 4   Preparation time: 15 mins   Cooking time: 2 hours

Crispy Seasoned Whitebait Myulchi Bokeum

These crisp, salty-sweet fish make a wonderful snack or appetizer that goes very well with beer or *soju*, or eaten with rice and kimchi.

1 tablespoon vegetable oil
2 cups (100 g) small whitebait
3 cloves garlic, crushed
1 thin slice ginger crushed or $1/_4$ teaspoon ginger grated
2 teaspoons water
1 tablespoon corn syrup, malt syrup or sugar syrup
$1/_2$ tablespoon toasted sesame seeds
Green chili, to garnish (optional)

1 Heat 1 teaspoon of the vegetable oil in a wok over medium heat and stir-fry the whitebait until crisp and cooked, about 5 minutes. Remove the whitebait from the wok and drain on paper towels. Clean the wok and set aside.
2 Place the garlic, ginger and water in a small bowl and mix to form a paste.
3 Heat the remaining vegetable oil in the cleaned wok over medium heat and stir-fry the blended paste for 1 minute. Add the whitebait and continue to stir-fry for another 2 minutes. Add the corn syrup and sesame seeds, and mix well. Garnish with the green chili and serve at room temperature.

Note: These small, sometimes tiny, whitebait are sold dried, freeze-dried or precooked. Another variety of whitebait, about 1 in ($2^1/_2$ cm) long, are available fresh, precooked or frozen and can be used for this recipe. However, they need to be shallow fried until crisp in step 1. Larger dried whitebaits (anchovies) may also be used, but remove the heads and bones beforehand.

Serves 4   Preparation time: 15 mins   Cooking time: 8 mins

Cold Stuffed Shrimp Daeha Naengche

This excellent appetizer of boiled shrimp with crunchy, refreshing strips of cucumber and nashi pear is best made with large shrimp and served with a tangy dressing. In the photo on the right, the shrimp are bound with long strips of jellyfish to the cucumber and nashi pear. However, blanched spring onion greens are easier to find and work just as well.

8 fresh large shrimp (10 oz/300 g), washed and drained
$1^1/_2$–2 cups (375–500 ml) water
1 spring onion, sliced
$^1/_2$ small onion, thinly sliced (optional)
4 lemon slices
3–in (8–cm) piece Japanese cucumber, sliced into thin, long strips
$^1/_2$ large nashi pear (about $1^3/_4$ cups/300 g), sliced into thin, long strips
8 spring onions, green part only, blanched to soften
  or strips of jellyfish

Vinegar Garlic Dressing
$^1/_4$ cup (60 ml) rice vinegar
1 tablespoon sugar
1 tablespoon lemon juice
4–6 cloves garlic, minced
1 teaspoon salt

1 Combine the Vinegar Garlic Dressing ingredients in a bowl and mix thoroughly. Set aside.
2 Peel off one section of the shell along the middle of the shrimp. Make a little incision and remove the intestinal tract. Skewer each shrimp lengthwise from the tail to the head with a bamboo skewer to prevent it from curling during cooking. Use a wide saucepan or a pot large enough to fit the skewers and add enough water to cover the shrimp. Add the spring onion, onion and lemon slices, and bring to a boil. Reduce the heat and simmer for 2 minutes.
3 Add the skewered shrimp and cook for 4 minutes, or until the shrimp turn pink and are cooked through. Drain and set aside to cool.
4 Remove the skewers and peel the shrimp, but leave the heads and tails intact. Slice the back of each shrimp and make a long slit along the underside of the shrimp.
5 Place strips of cucumber and pear on the underside of each shrimp, holding them in place with your hand. Secure them firmly with the softened spring onion greens or jellyfish and place each shrimp on a small plate. Pour the Vinegar Garlic Dressing over the shrimp and serve chilled or at room temperature.

Note: The crunchy texture of the jellyfish makes it ideal for cold salads. It is sold in rectangular pieces or cut into strips. If using, blanch in hot water for a few seconds and leave to soak in cold water until needed. Do not overcook as this would make the jellyfish very rubbery. Alternatively, the salad can be served in a bowl and simply tossed with the dressing. If nashi pear is not available, substitute with sliced pears, jicama or fresh water chestnuts.

Serves 4   Preparation time: 35 mins   Cooking time: 10 mins

Traditional Rice Flour Pancake Rolls   Milssam

Prepare these rolls with a tasty filling of beef, vegetables and omelet before bringing them to the table. For a more informal gathering, place everything separately on the table for everyone to help themselves.

Oil, to cook the pancakes
1 small zucchini, sliced into long, thin shreds
4 dried black Chinese mushrooms, soaked in water for 30 minutes, stems discarded and caps sliced into long shreds
1 small green bell pepper, thinly sliced into long shreds
1 small carrot, sliced into long shreds
$2/_3$ cup (65 g) slivered bamboo shoots
7 oz (200 g) beef, shredded
1 teaspoon salt
1 tablespoon sesame oil
5 teaspoons vegetable oil
3 tablespoons pine nuts, crushed

Batter
1 cup (125 g) rice flour
1 cup (125 g) glutinous rice flour
1 teaspoon salt
2 cups (500 ml) water

Vinegar Soy Dip
3 tablespoons soy sauce
$1^1/_2$ tablespoons rice vinegar
1 tablespoon water
$1/_2$ teaspoon sugar (optional)

1 Mix all the ingredients for the Vinegar Soy Dip in a bowl and set aside.
2 Prepare the Batter by combining all the ingredients. If desired, you can color the batter with a food coloring of your choice.
3 Lightly grease the bottom of a small skillet or crepe pan with a diameter of about 6 in (15 cm), wiping away the excess oil with a paper towel. Heat the skillet over low heat, add 2 tablespoons of the Batter and swirl to cover the bottom of the skillet. Cook over very low heat for 1 minute, then flip the pancake over and cook the other side. Repeat until all the Batter is used up. Cover the pancakes and set aside in a warm place.
4 Sprinkle a pinch of the salt and half a teaspoon of sesame oil over the zucchini. Repeat with the mushrooms, bell pepper, carrot, bamboo shoots and beef—sprinkling salt and sesame oil over all the vegetables and beef, but keeping them separate.
5 Heat 1 teaspoon of the vegetable oil in a wok and lightly stir-fry the zucchini for 30 seconds. Drain, then transfer the cooked zucchini to a plate. Repeat with the rest of the vegetables, heating 1 teaspoon of vegetable oil in the wok before lightly stir-frying each batch for 30 seconds. Drain and set the vegetables aside. Add the remaining vegetable oil and stir-fry the beef for 1 minute until the color changes. Set aside.
6 Place a little of the beef and vegetables onto the center of a pancake and roll up tightly. Sprinkle the crushed pine nuts and serve at room temperature with the Vinegar Soy Dip, and Mustard and Lemon Sauce (page 90).

Makes 25 pieces   Preparation time: 40 mins   Cooking time: 30 mins

Fresh Seafood and Spring Onion Pancakes
Pa Jeon

Pancakes are very popular in Korea, combining a mixture of basic ingredients in simple batter. As seafood is widely available in most parts of the country, pancakes made with oysters, fish or mixed seafood are often found. Plenty of spring onions add extra flavor to this version, made with fresh oysters.

$1/3$ cup (40 g) glutinous rice flour
$1/3$ cup (40 g) rice flour
$1/3$ cup (50 g) flour
1 large egg, lightly beaten
1 teaspoon salt
$1/2$ teaspoon ground white pepper
$3/4$ cup (185 ml) water
8 teaspoons vegetable oil
12–16 spring onions, cut into 6–in (15–cm) lengths,
  or length of the skillet
$1/2$ cup (100 g) fresh oysters, rinsed and drained
  or $3/4$ cup (150 g) mixed seafood, such as fish, clams, shrimps and squid,
  cut into small pieces
Generous pinch of dried chili strips, or 1 red chili, deseeded and sliced into
  long, thin strips (optional)

Garlic Soy Dip
3 tablespoons soy sauce
$1/2$–1 tablespoon rice vinegar
1 teaspoon minced garlic
$1/2$ teaspoon sesame oil
1 teaspoon toasted sesame seeds
$1/4$ teaspoon freshly ground black pepper

1 Mix all the ingredients for the dip in a bowl and set aside.
2 Combine the flours, egg, salt and white pepper in a mixing bowl, gradually stirring in the water to make a smooth, thin batter. Keep 4 tablespoons of the batter aside, then divide the rest of the batter into 4 portions.
3 Heat 2 teaspoons of the vegetable oil in a skillet (diameter of 6 in/15 cm). When the oil is moderately hot, add 1 portion of the batter and spread it over the base of the skillet to make a thin pancake.
4 Lay the spring onion sections in neat rows on the batter, then scatter the seafood and chili on top. Drizzle 1 tablespoon of the reserved batter over the spring onions and oysters to secure to the pancake. Cook for 2 to 3 minutes over medium heat until the pancake is golden brown underneath and the top starts to set. Turn the pancake over and cook for another minute. Repeat with the remaining portions of batter to make 4 pancakes. Serve hot with little bowls of the Garlic Soy Dip.

> Note: To save time, make 2 large pancakes in a 12–in (30–cm) skillet and slice spring onions to fit. For an equally delicious vegetarian Spring Onion Pancake, omit seafood and double the amount of spring onions.

Makes 4 pancakes   Preparation time: 10 mins   Cooking time: 20 mins

Pine Nut Rice Porridge   Jaotjuk

1/2 cup (100 g) uncooked short-grain
  rice, soaked in plenty of water for
  30 minutes, then drained
3 1/2 cups (875 ml) water
1/2 cup (75 g) pine nuts, finely
  ground
1/2 teaspoon salt

1 Place the drained rice and 2 cups (500 ml) of water in a blender. Pulse the blender until the rice is coarsely ground. Do not purée the rice.
2 Transfer the rice and ground pine nuts to a pot and add the remaining water. Bring to a boil over medium heat, stirring constantly. Lower the heat and simmer uncovered for 30 to 35 minutes, stirring several times, until the porridge is thick and cooked. Season with the salt and serve.

Serves 4   Preparation time: 5 minutes   Cooking time: 35 mins

Pumpkin Porridge   Hobakjuk

1 lb (500 g) peeled pumpkin, cut into
  small chunks
5 cups (1 1/4 liters) water
1/3 cup (40 g) rice flour
1–2 tablespoons soft brown sugar
1/2 teaspoon salt
2 tablespoons toasted pumpkin
  seeds or pine nuts (optional)

1 Place the pumpkin in a pot with 4 cups (1 liter) of water. Bring to a boil, cover, then reduce the heat and simmer for 25 minutes until the pumpkin is very soft and breaks up completely when stirred with a wooden spoon.
2 Mix the rice flour with the remaining cup of water, then add the mixture into the pot of softened pumpkin. Bring to a boil over medium heat, stirring constantly.
3 Reduce the heat and simmer for 2 minutes, then add the sugar and salt. Serve in individual bowls, topped with the toasted pumpkin seeds.

Serves 6–8   Preparation time: 10 mins   Cooking time: 30 mins

Abalone Rice Porridge   Jeonbokjuk

1 teaspoon sesame oil
1/2 cup (100 g) uncooked rice,
  soaked in 1 cup (250 ml) of water
  for 4 hours, then drained
3 cups (750 ml) water
8 oz (250 g) canned abalone or
  clams, drained and thinly sliced;
  reserve liquid from the can
1/2 teaspoon salt
4 egg yolks (optional)

1 Heat the sesame oil in a pot and stir-fry the drained rice, coating the grains thoroughly with the oil.
2 Add the water and the reserved cup of abalone liquid, and bring to a boil over medium heat. Reduce the heat and simmer, partially covered, for 30 to 40 minutes. Stir from time to time until the rice is cooked and very tender.
3 Set aside some abalone slices for garnish. Add the remaining abalone and salt. Remove from the heat and stir. Serve in 4 deep bowls, topped with the reserved abalone slices. The egg yolks can be served separately in small bowls to be added into the hot porridge if desired.

Serves 4   Preparation time: 4 hours   Cooking time: 45 mins

Chilled Summer Noodles with Beef and Vegetables   Mulnaemgmyeon

While a dish of chilled beef broth noodles with slivers of nashi pear and cucumbers may seem unusual, it is really very light and refreshing—a brief respite from the intense heat of the Korean summer.

7 oz (200 g) dried wheat or buckwheat (soba) noodles
6 cups (1$^1/_2$ liters) beef stock (page 42)
8 oz (250 g) brisket or chuck beef
1 in (2$^1/_2$ cm) ginger, sliced
1 medium onion, sliced
2–3 cloves garlic, crushed
8 in (20 cm) square dried kelp (*konbu*), washed
1$^1/_4$ teaspoons salt
$^1/_2$ large nashi pear (about 1$^3/_4$ cups/300 g), peeled and sliced into thin strips
2 hard-boiled eggs, halved lengthwise
Japanese mustard, to serve
Rice vinegar, to serve

Seasoned Vegetables
3 small Japanese cucumbers, sliced into thin, long strips
4 oz (125 g) daikon radish (about 2 in/5 cm), sliced into thin, long strips
2 pinches of salt
Pinch of minced garlic
Pinch of ground red pepper (optional)
Pinch of sesame seeds (optional)

1 Prepare the vegetables by seasoning the cucumbers with a pinch of salt. Set aside. Season the daikon with a pinch of salt, garlic, ground pepper and sesame seeds, and set aside.
2 Bring a pot of water to a boil, reduce the heat, drop in the noodles and simmer for 1 minute. Drain, then refresh the noodles immediately in a container of ice water.
3 Place the beef stock, brisket, ginger, onion and garlic in a pot and bring to a boil. Cover, then reduce the heat and simmer for 30 minutes. Add the dried kelp and continue to simmer for 1 hour, or until the beef is tender.
4 Discard the kelp, add the salt and remove from the heat. Leave the beef in the soup until cooled, then remove and slice it thin. Set the beef aside. Strain the soup and place both the soup and the beef in the refrigerator to chill. When the soup is cold, skim off the layer of fat on the surface.
5 Portion the noodles into 4 large bowls and garnish with the sliced beef, nashi pear and eggs. Top each bowl with the seasoned cucumbers and daikon, then pour the chilled soup over the noodles. Serve with Japanese mustard, vinegar and soy, accompanied with side dishes of Simple Daikon Salad (page 84) or Daikon Radish Kimchi (page 28) and Classic Chinese Cabbage Kimchi (page 27) if desired.

Serves 4   Preparation time: 20 mins   Cooking time: 1 hour 30 mins

Clam Soup   Daehaptang

2 lbs (1 kg) fresh small clams
4 cups (1 liter) water
7 oz (200 g) daikon radish (about
  3 in/8 cm), thinly sliced
4 cloves garlic, smashed
$1/4$ teaspoon grated ginger
$1/2$ teaspoon dried chili flakes
  or $1/2$ red chili, deseeded and sliced
  into thin strips (optional)
1 cup (75 g) bean sprouts (optional),
  tails discarded
$1/2$ spring onion, sliced, to garnish

1 Soak the clams in cool, lightly salted water for 20 minutes, then scrub with a brush. Place the clams into a pot, add the water and bring to a boil. Boil for about 7 minutes until the clams open, then remove from the heat and drain, reserving the clam stock and keeping the clams aside. Strain the stock carefully to remove any sand or grit. Rinse the pot well and return the strained stock to the pot. Check the clams to ensure that there is little or no grit inside them, then portion into 4 individual soup bowls.
2 Bring the clam stock to a boil and add the daikon, garlic, ginger, chili flakes or chili. Simmer for 5 minutes, or until the daikon is soft. Add salt if desired, then add the bean sprouts. Turn off the heat and ladle the soup over the clams and garnish with the spring onion.

Note: The cooked clam meat can be shelled before serving, and served separately without the soup.

Serves 4   Preparation time: 20 mins   Cooking time: 15 mins

Stuffed Steamed Clams   Daehap Jjim

4 fresh large clams or 1 lb (500 g)
  regular clams, scrubbed with a
  brush and soaked in lightly salted
  water for 20 minutes
$1/4$ cup (60 ml) water
1 clove garlic, minced
$1/4$ teaspoon sesame oil
$1/4$ teaspoon sugar
$1/4$ teaspoon ground white pepper
1 hard boiled egg, shelled, yolk and
  white separated
$1/2$ teaspoon minced parsley, to
  garnish
$1/2$ red chili, deseeded and minced,
  to garnish (optional)

1 Place the fresh clams and water in a pot and bring to a boil. Cook, stirring several times, until the clams start to open, about 7 minutes. Turn off the heat and drain the clams, reserving the clam juice. Strain the juice thoroughly to remove any sand or grit, and reserve 1 to 2 tablespoons of the juice.
2 Remove the clam meat from their shells, discarding the small muscle and keeping the larger clam shells. Mince the large clam meat, but leave the meat from the smaller clams whole. Place all the meat in a bowl and mix with the garlic, sesame oil, sugar and pepper.
3 Press the egg white through a coarse sieve. Set aside, then repeat with the egg yolk. Place the sieved egg white and yolk into the large clam shells, or onto small saucers, then top with the clam meat.
4 Heat the reserved clam juice and drizzle over the meat. Garnish with the parsley and chili, and serve.

Serves 4   Preparation time: 20 mins + 15 mins soaking time   Cooking time: 7 mins

Noodle Soup with Clams and Vegetables
Kalguksu

A delicate and easy dish to prepare, this noodle soup makes a satisfying light meal.

1 lb (500 g) baby clams
2 cups (500) ml water
3 cups (750 ml) beef stock (page 42) or chicken stock
1 medium potato, peeled and sliced into thin strips
1 medium onion, halved and bruised
1 medium zucchini, sliced into thin strips
2 cloves garlic, bruised
$^1/_2$ teaspoon salt
15 oz (450 g) fresh wheat or udon noodles,
  or 8 oz (250 g) dried buckwheat noodles
Dried chili flakes, to serve (optional)

Sauce
3 tablespoons soy sauce
1 red chili, finely minced
1 teaspoon minced ginger
2 teaspoons minced spring onion
1 teaspoon sesame oil
1 teaspoon toasted sesame seeds
1 tablespoon beef stock (page 42) (optional) or water

1 To make the Sauce, combine the ingredients and mix well. Pour into 4 small sauce bowls and set aside.
2 Scrub the clams and soak in lightly salted water. Bring the water to a boil, add the clams and cook for 3 minutes or until the shells open. Drain the clams, reserving the juice. Remove the clam meat, discard shells and set the meat aside.
3 To make the stock, combine the beef and clam stock in a large pot. Add the potato and onion, and simmer for 10 minutes until the potato is almost tender. Add the zucchini, garlic and salt, and simmer for 2 minutes. Discard the onion and garlic cloves, and keep the soup warm over low heat.
4 To cook fresh noodles, blanch in boiling water for 1 to 2 minutes until cooked. Dried noodles require about 5–7 minutes to soften, or see packet instructions. Drain the noodles and portion into 4 large bowls.
5 Increase the heat for the soup stock and add the clam meat. Stir and remove from the heat. Ladle the soup, clams and vegetables over the noodles. Serve hot with the Sauce and dried chili flakes.

Serves 4   Preparation time: 20 mins   Cooking time: 15 mins

Classic Kimchi Stew with Beef and Tofu Kimchi Jjigae

The liberal amount of ground red pepper in this satisfying soup is excellent for clearing the nasal passages, and is regarded by many as a remedy for the symptoms of the common cold in Korea. Even without a cold, you can still enjoy this tangy dish, which is somewhere between a soup and a stew. Eaten with steamed rice, it's a meal on its own. The stew is usually served in a cast iron, clay or stoneware pot which can be placed over direct heat.

2 teaspoons vegetable oil
8 oz (250 g) beef sirloin, thinly sliced
  or boneless pork ribs, sliced
1/2 large onion, thinly sliced
1–2 teaspoons minced garlic
2 cups (350 g) sliced kimchi and
  3/4 cup (185 ml) kimchi juice
3 1/2 cups (875 ml) beef stock
  (page 42)
8 oz (250 g) firm tofu, thickly sliced
2–4 teaspoons ground red pepper
1 tablespoon soy sauce
1–2 teaspoons sugar
1 leek, sliced diagonally
2 spring onions, sectioned
1 red or green chili, sliced

1 Heat the oil in a pot and stir-fry the beef until it changes color. Add the onion, garlic, kimchi and stir-fry for 2 to 3 minutes. Add the beef stock and bring to a boil, then reduce the heat and simmer for another minute.
2 Add the kimchi juice, tofu, red pepper, soy sauce, sugar and leek. Return the soup to a boil and cook for 2 minutes, then sprinkle the spring onions and sliced chili. Serve hot.

Note: To cut thin slices of beef, wrap the meat in plastic wrap and chill it in the freezer for 30 minutes before slicing with a sharp knife. For a robust flavor, increase the amount of kimchi juice, soy sauce and sugar, if desired.

Serves 4   Preparation time: 10 mins   Cooking time: 5 mins

Vegetables and Tofu Simmered in Bean Paste Doenjang Jjigae

5 oz (150 g) sirloin beef, thinly sliced
8 fresh mushrooms
1 small zucchini, sliced
1 small bell pepper (optional),
  cut into bite-sized pieces
4 oz (125 g) firm tofu, cubed
16 fresh small clams (4 oz/125 g)
1 red chili, sliced, to garnish
1 spring onion, thinly sliced, to garnish

Bean Paste Stock
3-in (8–cm) square dried kelp (*konbu*)
2 heaped tablespoons dried whitebait
8 oz (250 g) daikon radish (about
  4 in/10 cm), sliced
8 spring onions, cut into lengths
3 cloves garlic, peeled and bruised
5 pieces sliced ginger
1–2 teaspoons ground red pepper
6 cups (1$^1/_2$ liters) water
3$^1/_2$ tablespoons chili bean paste
  (*gochujang*)
5 tablespoons soybean paste
  (*deonjang*)

1 Place all the ingredients for the Bean Paste Stock, except for the bean pastes, in a pot and bring to a boil for about 15 minutes. Lower the heat, add the bean pastes and simmer for 5 minutes. Strain, reserve the stock and discard the solids.
2 Return the stock to the pot, increase the heat and add the beef, mushrooms, zucchini, bell pepper and tofu, and bring to almost a boil. Simmer for 5 minutes, or until the vegetables are cooked.
3 Add the clams and simmer until they open. Garnish with the chili and spring onion, and serve hot as a side dish.

Note: If serving this dish as a one-pot meal, increase the amount of mushroom, zucchini, bell pepper, tofu and beef. Canned abalone and clams, and its juice, may also be added for extra flavor.

Serves 4   Preparation time: 20 mins   Cooking time: 35 mins

Spicy Beef Soup   Yukgaejang

This tangy, piping hot soup is a favorite on hot summer days in Korea. This may seem strange, but Koreans believe that the liberal amount of chili encourages perspiration, thus cooling the body. Even if you serve this in the middle of winter, you'll find it a robust soup, ideal with rice.

1 lb (500 g) beef flank or shin beef, halved
6 cups (1^1/$_2$ liters) water
1 portion Prepared Bracken (see recipe below) or 3 cups (150 g) chopped spinach, blanched in boiling water to soften
2 cups (150 g) bean sprouts, tails discarded
2 leeks, halved lengthwise and cut into lengths
2 eggs, lightly beaten

Seasoning
1 tablespoon soy sauce
1^1/$_2$ teaspoons crushed garlic
4 teaspoons ground red pepper
1^1/$_2$ teaspoons chili bean paste (gochujang)
1 teaspoon sesame oil
^{1}/$_2$ teaspoon sugar
^{1}/$_2$ teaspoon salt

1 Combine the ingredients for the Seasoning and set aside.
2 Place the beef and water in a pot and bring to a boil. Cover, then reduce the heat and simmer for about 1^1/$_2$ hours until the beef is tender. Remove the beef from the pot and allow to cool.
3 Bring the beef broth to a boil over medium-low heat, cover, and leave to simmer. Shred the cooled beef very finely.
4 If using spinach instead of bracken, mix the softened spinach with ^{1}/$_2$ teaspoon soy sauce and 1 teaspoon peeled and crushed garlic, mix well and set aside.
5 Combine the Seasoning with the bracken and shredded beef. Add the beef, bracken, bean sprouts and leeks to the simmering broth and allow to heat through, about 5 minutes. Just before serving, pour the beaten eggs slowly into the soup, stirring gently at the same time. Remove from the heat immediately and serve with bowls of steaming hot rice.

Serves 4   Preparation time: 15 mins   Cooking time: 2 hours

Prepared Bracken

1^1/$_2$ cups (20 g) dried bracken
Pinch of salt
1 teaspoon soy sauce
1 teaspoon garlic, finely diced
1 teaspoon oil
^{1}/$_4$ cup (60 ml) water
^{1}/$_2$ teaspoon sesame oil

1 Rinse the dried bracken and soak in water overnight. Drain and season with the salt, soy sauce, garlic and oil. Mix well.
2 Heat a small skillet and stir-fry the seasoned bracken for 2 minutes. Add the water and stir-fry on medium heat until dry, about 3 minutes.
3 Remove the bracken from the heat. Drizzle the sesame oil and mix well.

Note: Alternatively, dried bracken can be rinsed and boiled in water for 30 to 45 minutes to soften.

Makes 2 cups   Preparation time: 5 mins + overnight marinating time
Cooking time: 5 mins

Ginseng Chicken Soup with Rice and Chestnut Stuffing   Samgyetang

Ginseng is one of Korea's most famous products—valued for its all-encompassing goodness as a booster for the immune system. A source of energy and vitality, it promotes longevity and increases libido. Aged ginseng is used for preparing tonics. There are different grades of ginseng, the top grade being wild Korean ginseng, which is considered to be the best. The fresh cream-colored roots are blended for drinks and used for cooking.

2 spring chickens (1 lb/500 g each), or 1 large chicken (3 lbs/$1^1/_2$ kg)
2 pieces finger-thick fresh ginseng roots, washed
  or 3 tablespoons dried ginseng shavings
  or 4 tablespoons dried ginseng roots and tails
1 teaspoon salt
$^1/_4$ teaspoon ground white pepper
2 dried red dates
2 thin slices ginger
8 cloves garlic, peeled and left whole
1 leek, green part only, or spring onions sliced diagonally, to garnish

Stuffing
$^1/_2$ cup (100 g) glutinous rice, soaked in boiling water for 30 minutes,
  then drained
4 dried red dates
4 chestnuts (optional)
$^1/_2$ teaspoon salt

Salt and Pepper Dip
1 tablespoon salt
1 teaspoon freshly ground black pepper

1 Combine the ingredients for the Stuffing and mix well. Divide the mixture into two portions and set aside.
2 Combine the Salt and Pepper Dip ingredients. Set aside.
3 Rinse the chickens inside and out, then pat dry with paper towels. Stuff the chickens with the Stuffing, but do not pack the mixture too tightly as it will swell during cooking. If using 2 chickens, portion the Stuffing into two. Close the cavity of the chicken by threading a skewer in and out of the flap.
4 Place the chickens in a pot large enough to hold the chickens, then add enough water to cover. Add the ginseng, salt, pepper, dried red dates, ginger and garlic, and bring to a boil. Cover, then reduce the heat and simmer gently. Turn the chicken and continue to cook until the chicken is very tender and the flesh is almost falling off the bone; about another 40 to 50 minutes for 2 spring chickens or 1 hour for a large chicken.
5 To serve, remove the chicken from the pot and cut into halves or quarters. Return the chicken to the soup and serve in bowls. If preferred, serve the soup in small bowls and the chicken on a separate platter and garnish with the leek. Serve with the Salt and Pepper Dip, and bowls of kimchi on the side.

Serves 4–6   Preparation time: 15 mins   Cooking time: 1 hour 30 mins

Soft Tofu Soup with Pork   Sundubu Jjigae

This spicy and wholesome soup is kept piping hot in the traditional hotpot (*ttukbaegi*). The food is simmered in the hotpot directly over an open fire, and the pot transferred to the dining table. A fresh egg or two is cracked and stirred into the soup just before serving, accompanied with rice, side dishes and an array of kimchi.

10 oz (300 g) pork collar or pork ribs, diced
1 teaspoon oil
1 teaspoon ground red pepper, or more to taste
1¹/₂ cups (225 g) coarsely chopped kimchi
1 lb (500 g) silken tofu, mashed into pieces with a fork
1 teaspoon salt
1–2 tablespoons soy sauce
1 leek, green portion only, sliced diagonally
2 eggs (optional)
1 spring onion, sliced, to garnish

Stock
5 cups (1¹/₄ liters) water
3–in (8–cm) square dried kelp (*konbu*)
¹/₂ onion, sliced

Pork Marinade
1 teaspoon minced garlic
1 teaspoon ground red pepper
1 teaspoon soy sauce
¹/₂ teaspoon sesame oil
¹/₂ teaspoon sugar

1 Place the Stock ingredients in a pot and bring to a boil. Reduce the heat to low and simmer for 10 minutes, or until the stock reduces to 4 cups (1 liter). Strain the stock, discard the solids and set the stock aside.
2 Combine the Pork Marinade and pork in a small bowl and mix well.
3 Heat the oil in a medium pot and stir-fry the ground red pepper for a few seconds. Add the pork and kimchi, and continue to stir-fry for 2 to 3 minutes. Add the stock and bring to a boil. Reduce the heat and simmer for 20 minutes, or until the pork is tender. Add the mashed tofu and continue to simmer for another 5 minutes.
4 Add more ground red pepper if you prefer more heat, then add the salt and soy sauce, and simmer for 10 minutes. Add the leek and stir. If desired, break the 2 eggs into the soup and garnish with the spring onion. Serve immediately.

Serves 4   Preparation time: 20 mins   Cooking time: 45 hour

Pollack Soup with Daikon   Bukoh Congnamul Guk

1 teaspoon sesame oil and 1 teaspoon vegetable oil
1 whole dried pollack ($2^{1}/_{2}$ oz/80 g), deboned, head and tail discarded, and
  sliced into bite-sized pieces
  or shaved strips of Korean dried cod (about $2^{1}/_{2}$ oz/80 g)
1 cup (75 g) bean sprouts (optional), tails discarded
$^{1}/_{2}$ teaspoon salt (optional)
$^{1}/_{4}$ teaspoon ground white pepper
1 egg, lightly beaten with a pinch of salt
$^{1}/_{2}$ red or green chili, thinly sliced, to garnish
1 spring onion, sliced, to garnish
Ground red pepper, to serve

Stock
1 leek, thinly sliced
1 piece dried kelp (*konbu*) (3 x 6–in/8 x 15–cm)
$^{3}/_{4}$ in (2 cm) ginger, peeled and bruised
6 cloves garlic, peeled and bruised
5 cups ($1^{1}/_{4}$ liters) water
7 oz (200 g) daikon radish (about 3 in/8 cm), halved and sliced

1 Place the Stock ingredients into a pot and bring to a boil. Reduce the heat and simmer for 15 minutes. Strain and reserve the stock and daikon, and discard all the other ingredients. Return the stock to the pot and keep warm.
2 Heat the sesame and vegetable oil in a frying pan and stir-fry the dried fish for 1 minute.
3 Bring the Stock to a boil, add the fish and simmer for 3 minutes. Add the bean sprouts and stir. Season with the salt and pepper, then slowly pour the beaten egg into the soup while stirring gently. Garnish with the sliced chili and spring onion. Serve hot with a small dish of the ground red pepper.

Note: Taste this dish before adding more salt. When using Korean dried pollack or cod shavings, do not wash or soak the fish in water. If using other types of salt cod, slice and soak the fish overnight in water. Drain and squeeze dry before use.

Serves 4–6   Preparation time: 10 mins   Cooking time: 18 mins

Stuffed Tofu and Beef Casserole Sogogi Dubu Jeongol

7 oz (200 g) lean ground beef
$1/2$ teaspoon sesame oil
$1/2$ teaspoon minced garlic
$1/4$ teaspoon salt
$1/4$ teaspoon freshly ground black
  pepper
2 large cakes of firm tofu (8 oz/250 g
  each)
$1/4$ cup (60 ml) vegetable oil
8 chrysanthemum leaves (optional)
Dried kelp, cut into 8 long strips,
  blanched to soften, for tying
7 oz (200 g) beef sirloin, cut into 8
  thin slices
$1/2$ red bell pepper, sliced
  or 1 red chili, sliced
$1/2$ teaspoon ground red pepper
4 cups (1 liter) beef stock (page 42)
1 egg yolk, lightly beaten (optional)

1 Place the ground beef in a small bowl and add the sesame oil, garlic, salt and pepper. Mix well and set aside.
2 Cut each piece of the tofu into 4 pieces and pat dry with paper towels. Heat the oil in a wok and fry the tofu until it is golden brown on all sides, turning the tofu carefully to prevent it from breaking up. Drain on paper towels and cool. Halve each piece horizontally.
3 Divide the ground beef into 8 portions and shape into the same size as the tofu. To assemble, place a portion of beef on a piece of tofu, then top with a second piece of tofu and a chrysanthemum leaf if using. Tie each tofu "sandwich" with a softened kelp.
4 Arrange the tofu in a heatproof casserole dish and add the beef sirloin slices, bell pepper and ground red pepper. Add the beef stock, bring to a boil, then cover and simmer gently for 10 minutes. Add the beaten egg yolk and serve hot.

Note: If kelp is not available, substitute spring onions and use only the green portions.

Serves 4   Preparation time: 20 mins   Cooking time: 15 mins

Mushroom Casserole Beosot Jeongol

1 lb (500 g) mixed fresh mushrooms
  (enoki, oyster and button)
10 fresh shiitake mushrooms
2–3 leaves Chinese cabbage, cut into
  small sections
$1/2$ red bell pepper, cut into strips
4 cups (1 liter) beef stock (page 42)
2 cloves garlic, minced
7 oz (200 g) beef sirloin or boneless
  chicken breast, thinly sliced
1 leek, green part only, thinly sliced
$1^1/2$ teaspoons salt
$1/2$ teaspoon ground black pepper

1 Discard the tough mushroom stems and slice the caps into thick strips. Place the mushrooms, cabbage and bell pepper in a heatproof casserole dish or pot.
2 Bring the stock to a boil in a deep saucepan over medium heat and add the mushrooms.
3 Pour the stock into the casserole dish or pot, then add the garlic. Return the stock to a boil slowly, then reduce the heat and simmer for 7 minutes. Add the sliced beef and continue to simmer for another 3 minutes. Add the leek and stir. Season with the salt and pepper, and serve hot with steamed rice.

Note: If not using beef, substitute with boneless chicken breast and chicken stock.

Serves 4   Preparation time: 20 mins   Cooking time: 10 mins

Crab and Vegetable Hotpot Kkotgetang

A delicious, warming seafood dish, ideal for cold winter evenings.

2 lbs (1 kg) fresh flower crabs or crab claws
20 clams (5 oz/150 g), soaked in lightly salted water for 20 minutes,
  and scrubbed with a brush
2 tablespoons soybean paste (*deonjang*)
1 tablespoon chili bean paste (*gochujang*)
7 cups (1^3/$_4$ liters) water
7 oz (200 g) daikon radish (about 3 in/8 cm), halved lengthwise and quartered
1 tablespoon soy sauce
2 slices ginger, minced
1 tablespoon ground red pepper
1 tablespoon minced garlic
1^1/$_2$ teaspoons salt
1–2 red or green chilies, deseeded and sliced
1 small leek, white part only, thinly sliced
2 bunches chrysanthemum greens (*tung ho*) or Chinese celery leaves, sliced

1 Clean and quarter the crabs. Crack open the crab claws to allow the flavors to penetrate.
2 Mix the soybean and chili bean paste with 1 cup (250 ml) water, then mash and strain into a large pot. Add the remaining water to the pot and simmer over medium high heat for 5 minutes.
3 Add the daikon, crab, soy sauce and ginger to the boiling stock, and simmer for 7–10 minutes on medium high heat.
4 Add the red pepper, garlic, salt and clams, stir and simmer for another 3 minutes, or until the clams are cooked and the shells open.
5 Add the chilies, leek and chrysanthemum greens or Chinese celery leaves, and leave to cook for another minute. Remove from the heat and serve with rice and pan-fried sweet green chili or other fried foods.

Note: Substitute fresh crabs with precooked crab claws or jumbo shrimp. If using, add this into the pot during the last 3 minutes of cooking.
If using live crabs such as Dungeness or mudcrabs, put a crab on a chopping board belly-side up. Place a heavy knife over its belly and hit the knife with a mallet to cut through the crab. (Be careful when handling live crabs as its pincers and claws can leave you with a very nasty wound.)
Lift the triangular-shaped "apron" on the underside of the crab. Insert your thumb between the body and topshell at the rear of crab, and pull the carapace off. Discard the grey gills and any green or spongy grey matter on the body. Clean thoroughly, then rinse and drain. Quarter the crabs and crack the claws so the flavors can penetrate.

Serves 4–6   Preparation time: 30 mins   Cooking time: 30 mins

Shrimp, Fish and Vegetable Hotpot Shinseolo

Shinseolo is a royal dish, served with only the best and freshest foods of the season. There are many ingredients in this communal one-pot meal shared in the company of good friends. Traditionally, the metallic hotpot is fired with charcoal. Nowadays, clutter-free electric hotpots are the way to go. Whichever you use, the result will be an excellent meal.

8 oz (250 g) daikon radish (about 4 in/10 cm), halved lengthwise and sliced
1 zucchini, sectioned and sliced lengthwise
8–12 medium fresh shrimp, peeled and deveined
2 leeks, sectioned
1 red chili, deseeded and cut into lengths (optional)
20–25 shelled gingko nuts
8 dried chestnuts, soaked in warm water for 30 minutes, and boiled for 30 minutes (optional)
1 tablespoon pine nuts
2 cloves garlic, minced
2 teaspoons sesame oil
4 cups (1 liter) beef stock (page 42) or water

Fried Vegetables
1 small carrot, peeled, sectioned and sliced lengthwise
4–8 large fresh mushrooms (shiitake, brown or oyster), thickly sliced
8 oz (250 g) firm tofu, sliced
$1/2$ cup (75 g) plain flour
1 egg, beaten
Oil for shallow frying

Meatballs
7 oz (200 g) minced chicken, pork or beef
2 cloves garlic, crushed
$1/2$ teaspoon sesame oil
$1/2$ teaspoon salt
$1/2$ teaspoon pepper
3 tablespoons flour
1 egg, beaten
Oil, for shallow frying

1 Dredge the carrot in the flour and shake off any excess flour. Heat the oil in a deep saucepan until very hot. Dip the carrot in the egg and fry until light golden brown, about 2 to 3 minutes, then remove and drain on paper towels. Repeat with the mushrooms and tofu, first coating in flour, then dipping in egg, and shallow fry. Drain and set aside.
2 To prepare the Meatballs, season the meat with the garlic, sesame oil, salt and pepper, and mix well. Pinch about 1 heaped teaspoon of minced meat and roll to form small balls. Dredge the Meatballs in the flour and coat with the egg. Heat the oil in the same saucepan and fry the Meatballs until light golden brown. Drain and set aside.
3 Arrange, in an alternate fashion, the daikon, zucchini, shrimp, leeks, chili and the Fried Vegetables in the moat of a hotpot. Top with the gingko nuts and cooked chestnuts, if using. Sprinkle the pine nuts, garlic and sesame oil.
4 Bring the beef stock to a boil in a large saucepan and pour it gently down the side of the hotpot. Simmer until the shrimp are cooked, about 10 to 15 minutes. If using an electrical hotpot, reduce the heat to medium. Diners can help themselves to the meat and vegetables with chopsticks, and when the ingredients have all been eaten, spoon the flavorsome soup into large soup bowls for everyone to enjoy. Although not traditional, you can serve this hotpot dish with Garlic Soy Dip (page 48).

Note: If you do not have a hotpot, use a heatproof casserole. Arrange all the ingredients in an alternating fashion. Pour the steaming hot beef stock gently down the side of the casserole. Simmer for 5 minutes to cook the shrimp and serve immediately. For more variety, use sliced fish (prepared like the Fried Vegetables) or chopped liver (prepared the same way as the Meatballs).

Serves 4   Preparation time: 1 hour 30 mins   Cooking time: 30 mins

Mixed Seafood Hotpot Haemul Jeongol

This spicy mixture of seafood is generally served in the dish in which it is cooked, with everyone helping themselves to morsels of crab, octopus, shrimp and clam, together with some of the rich stock. This is best accompanied by bowls of warm water topped with slices of lemon to freshen the hands.

1 fresh crab or 1 lb (500 g) cooked crab claws
10 oz (300 g) squid or octopus, cut into bite-sized pieces
8 fresh scallops
8 medium shrimp, peeled and deveined
12 medium clams or 1 lb (500 g) fresh, small clams, soaked in water
  for 20 minutes and scrubbed with a brush
2 medium abalone (optional)
4 large Chinese cabbage leaves (4 oz/125 g), cut into squares
1 cake soft tofu (8 oz/250 g), cubed
2 spring onions, cut into lengths
1 bunch chrysanthemum greens (*tung ho*) or watercress
2 red or green chilies, sliced (optional)
1 teaspoon ground red pepper

Fragrant Seafood Stock
6 cups (1^1/$_2$ liters) water
12 fresh mussels, scrubbed and cleaned
3–in (8–cm) square dried kelp (*konbu*)
1 leek, white part only, sliced
7 cloves garlic, crushed
2 teaspoons grated ginger
2 tablespoons chili bean paste (*gochujang*)
^{1}/$_2$–1 teaspoon ground red pepper
1 red or green chili, halved lengthwise
2 teaspoons salt

1 Place all the Fragrant Seafood Stock ingredients in a pot and bring to a boil. Reduce the heat and simmer for 15 minutes. Strain, reserve the stock and discard the solids. Keep the stock warm on low heat.
2 Lift the triangular-shaped "apron" on the underside of the crab. Insert your thumb between the body and topshell at the rear of crab, and pull the carapace off. Discard the grey gills and any green or spongy grey matter on the body. Clean thoroughly, then rinse and drain. Quarter the crabs and crack the claws so the flavors can penetrate.
3 Put the crab, squid, scallops, shrimp, clams, abalone, cabbage leaves and tofu in a large casserole dish or pot. Carefully pour the warm Fragrant Seafood Stock over the contents and bring to a boil. Cover and simmer for 5 minutes until cooked. Remove from the heat, then add the spring onions, chrysanthemum greens and chilies. Sprinkle the ground red pepper and serve with bowls of steamed rice and Vinegar Soy Dip (page 47) if desired.

Serves 6   Preparation time: 45 mins   Cooking time: 25 mins

Fish and Vegetable Hotpot   Urukmaeuntang

4 cups (1 liter) water
1 tablespoon ground red pepper
5 cloves garlic, peeled and left whole
2 teaspoons grated ginger
1$^1/_2$ teaspoons salt
7 oz (200 g) daikon radish (about 3 in/8 cm), halved and thickly sliced
1 zucchini, thickly sliced
1 small onion, thickly sliced
1 leek, cut into sections
10 oz (300 g) fresh salmon or other fresh fish fillets, cut into large pieces
8 oz (250 g) firm tofu, thickly sliced
1 red chili, deseeded and diagonally sliced
1 spring onion, cut into lengths, to garnish
1 bunch chrysanthemum greens (*tung ho*) or Chinese celery leaves
$^1/_2$ teaspoon ground white pepper (optional)
Dried chili strips, to garnish (optional)

1 Place the water, ground pepper, garlic, ginger, salt and daikon in a pot and bring to a boil. Reduce the heat and simmer for 5 minutes. Add the zucchini, onion and leek, and simmer for another 3 minutes.
2 Add the fish pieces, simmer for 5 minutes, then add the tofu and chili. Simmer for 1 to 2 minutes until the fish is just cooked. Add the spring onion and half of the chrysanthemum greens. Sprinkle the white pepper (if using), and garnish with the rest of the chrysanthemum greens and the dried chili strips.

Serves 4   Preparation time: 20 mins   Cooking time: 20 mins

Beef Bulgogi

Traditional *bulgogi* is made by cooking very thin strips of marinated beef over a charcoal fire using a special domed griddle with holes. These days, it is more likely to be cooked on a tabletop gas grill or in a cast iron skillet in the kitchen. If possible, barbecue the beef over wood or charcoal to get that good old-fashioned flavor. Thanks to the excellent marinade, the meat will still taste good when cooked in a skillet or frying pan.

1¹/₂ lbs (750 g) sirloin or rib eye beef, thinly sliced
1 onion, sliced
1 leek, diagonally sliced into very thin strips
8 fresh shiitake mushrooms, stems discarded and caps sliced (optional)
Toasted sesame seeds, to garnish

Bulgogi Marinade
1¹/₂–2 tablespoons minced garlic,
4–5 tablespoons soy sauce
2 tablespoons soft brown sugar
2 tablespoons corn syrup or sugar syrup
¹/₂ teaspoon freshly ground black pepper
2 tablespoons rice wine or sake
1 tablespoon sesame oil
1 large nashi pear (about 3¹/₂ cups/600 g), grated
2 spring onions, finely sliced
¹/₂ cup (125 ml) beef stock (page 42) (optional)

1 Mix all the Bulgogi Marinade ingredients together and combine with the beef in a large bowl. Cover and marinate for 2 hours.
2 Heat a large skillet or frying pan, add the beef, onion, leek and mushrooms, and stir-fry over high heat for about 4 minutes, or until the beef is cooked.
3 Garnish with the sesame seeds. Serve with chili bean paste (*gochujang*), lettuce leaves, sesame leaves, sliced raw garlic and sliced green chili on the side. Arrange these ingredients and the meat on a leaf, then wrap and dip the parcel in a spicy sauce before eating.

Note: Wrap the beef in plastic wrap and chill in the freezer for 30 minutes. Remove the plastic wrap and slice the beef very thinly, and then into strips. An alternative way of preparing this dish is to heat a barbecue or grill and cook the beef over high heat.

Serves 4   Preparation time: 20 mins + 2 hours marinating time
Cooking time: 5 mins

Fried Kimchi Rice with Beef   Kimchi Bokeumbap

This is a handy way of using leftover cooked rice, which can be kept refrigerated in a covered container (in fact, rice kept overnight is best for all fried rice dishes, as the rice is completely dry). In this recipe, the rice is stir-fried with shredded beef, spicy kimchi, onion, spring onions and garlic, and seasoned with soy sauce and sesame oil for a quick and tasty dish. Ideal for a light lunch or supper.

7 oz (200 g) ground beef or beef sirloin, cut into thin strips
$1^1/_2$ tablespoons soy sauce
2 cloves garlic, peeled and crushed
1 tablespoon vegetable oil
$^1/_2$ teaspoon sugar
1 small onion, diced
1 cup (250 g) firmly packed, sliced kimchi
3 cups (600 g) cold cooked rice, preferably short-grain rice
1 small bell pepper, diced (optional)
3 spring onions, thinly sliced
1 green chili, sliced
1 tablespoon sesame oil
Black sesame seeds, to garnish

1 Season the beef in a bowl with the soy sauce and garlic, mix well and leave to marinate for 5 minutes.
2 Heat $^1/_2$ tablespoon of the oil in a wok over high heat and stir-fry the beef with the sugar, onion and kimchi until the onion softens, about 1 to 2 minutes. Remove from the wok and set aside.
3 Reduce the heat to medium, add the remaining oil to the wok and heat until the oil is very hot. Add the rice and stir-fry for 30 seconds, then add the beef, bell pepper, spring onions and chili. Stir-fry until heated through, then transfer to a serving bowl and drizzle the sesame oil. Garnish with the black sesame seeds and serve.

Serves 4–6   Preparation time: 15 mins   Cooking time: 10 mins

Transparent Noodles with Beef and Vegetables   Japchae

A delicious and simple recipe, this popular party dish is also ideal for lunch or as a light meal.

10 oz (300 g) rib eye or other beef
  fillet, cut into thin strips
3 tablespoons vegetable oil
1 large egg, lightly beaten

Marinade
1 tablespoon soy sauce
1 tablespoon sugar
2 teaspoons sesame oil
3 cloves garlic, peeled and crushed
5 spring onions, cut into lengths

Noodles
1 packet (10 oz/300 g) dried sweet
  potato starch noodles
  or thick Chinese glass noodles
1 tablespoon soy sauce
1–2 tablespoons sugar
1 tablespoon sesame oil
1 teaspoon salt
$1/_4$ teaspoon ground white pepper

Vegetables
1 onion, thinly sliced
4 dried black Chinese mushrooms,
  rinsed, soaked in hot water for 30
  minutes to soften, stems discarded
  and caps thinly sliced
$1/_2$ cup (15 g) small dried wood ear
  mushrooms, rinsed, soaked in hot
  water for 10 minutes to soften, then
  cut into thin strips
1 carrot, cut in sections, then into
  thin strips
1 medium zucchini, cut in sections,
  then into thin strips
1 red or green bell pepper, cut into
  thin strips
1 tablespoon soy sauce
$1/_2$ teaspoon salt
$1/_2$ cup (125 ml) water

1 Combine the beef and the Marinade, mix well and set aside for 30 minutes.
2 Bring a pot of water to a boil and cook the noodles for 8 minutes (see packet instructions). Drain well, season with the soy sauce, sugar, sesame oil, salt and pepper, and set aside.
3 Heat $1/_2$ tablespoon of the oil in a skillet and add the egg. Swirl the egg to make a very thin omelet. Slice the cooked egg into long, thin strips and set aside to garnish.
4 Heat 1 tablespoon of the oil in the same skillet over high heat and stir-fry the beef until cooked, about 2 to 3 minutes, then set aside.
5 To prepare the Vegetables, heat the remaining oil in a wok over medium heat. Add the onion and stir-fry until transparent. Add the mushrooms and stir-fry for 2 minutes. Then increase the heat slightly and add the carrot, zucchini and bell pepper. Stir-fry for another 2 minutes. Add the soy sauce, salt and water. Stir-fry until the Vegetables are tender and the liquid has evaporated.
6 Toss the Noodles, Vegetables and beef together. Garnish with the thinly sliced fried egg and serve.

Note: Substitute beef with pressed tofu for an equally tasty vegetarian dish.

Serves 4–6   Preparation time: 35 mins + 30 mins marinating time   Cooking time: 15 mins

Bibimbap   Rice with Beef and Vegetables

Bibimbap is a healthy and hearty everyday dish of steamed rice, vegetables and meat. It is a meal on its own. When dished into a preheated hotpot, the rice forms a crispy crust at the bottom. Add a dollop of *gochujang,* mix it all up, and enjoy!

4 cups (800 g) freshly cooked short-grain rice, kept hot
Chili bean paste (*gochujang*), to serve

Seasoned Vegetables
1 zucchini, sectioned and cut into thin strips
1 carrot, sectioned and cut into thin strips
10 oz (300 g) spinach leaves, sliced
2 cups (150 g) soybean or mung bean sprouts, tails discarded
1 teaspoon crushed garlic
1 teaspoon sesame oil
1 teaspoon salt
1 portion Prepared Bracken (page 60) (optional)

Beef
8 oz (250 g) ground beef or very thinly sliced sirloin beef
2 teaspoons soy sauce
1 teaspoon garlic
1 teaspoon sesame oil
1 teaspoon sugar
$1/2$ teaspoon freshly ground black pepper

Simple Daikon Salad
8 oz (250 g) daikon radish (about 4 in/10 cm), halved, sliced into thin strips
$3/4$–1 tablespoon ground red pepper
1 teaspoon minced garlic
$3/4$ teaspoon salt
1 teaspoon brown sugar
1 teaspoon toasted sesame seeds
$1/4$ teaspoon sesame oil (optional)

1 Prepare the Seasoned Vegetables by bringing a pot of water to a boil and blanching the zucchini. Drain, then toss the zucchini in $1/4$ teaspoon garlic, $1/4$ teaspoon sesame oil and $1/4$ teaspoon salt. Repeat with the carrot, spinach and soybean sprouts, keeping them separate.
2 To make the daikon salad, combine the daikon and ground pepper, and mix well. Toss the daikon gently with the remaining ingredients and set aside.
3 Combine the ingredients for the Beef and mix well. Heat a nonstick skillet or wok over high heat and dry-fry the ground beef for 2 to 3 minutes until the color changes. Remove from the heat and set aside.
4 Scoop the hot cooked rice into 4 bowls, top each bowl with a portion of the vegetables, Prepared Bracken, seasoned ground beef and daikon, and serve with chili bean paste on the side.

Note: If desired, a fried egg, sunny-side up, can be placed on top of the rice before serving. If individual heatproof casserole dishes are available, grease the inside lightly with oil, add the rice and place over high heat for 3 minutes to sear the rice. Seasoned mushrooms or bamboo shoots are equally delicious with this dish (see recipe on page 31). Serve with the Simple Daikon Salad.

Serves 4   Preparation time: 60 mins   Cooking time: 10 mins

Grilled Beef Ribs Galbi Gui

2 lbs (1 kg) beef short ribs, cut into
  1$\frac{1}{2}$–in (4–cm) lengths

Marinade
2 tablespoons garlic, peeled and
  crushed
1 teaspoon grated ginger
$\frac{1}{4}$ cup (60 ml) soy sauce
1 tablespoon honey
4 tablespoons soft brown sugar
$\frac{1}{2}$ teaspoon freshly ground black
  pepper
2 tablespoons rice wine or sake
1$\frac{1}{2}$ tablespoons sesame oil
1 large nashi pear (about 3$\frac{1}{2}$
  cups/600 g), grated
2 spring onions, minced

1 If using frozen ribs, the bones may be dark red in color. If so place the ribs in cold water and soak for 20 minutes. Drain and squeeze the ribs gently to remove excess water.
2 Combine all the Marinade ingredients together, except the spring onions. Add the Marinade to the beef ribs and mix well. Then add the spring onions and toss lightly. Cover and marinate for at least 4 hours.
3 Heat a grill or broiler and grill the ribs for 3 to 4 minutes on each side, or until browned and cooked through. Serve with lettuce, perilla leaves, raw garlic and chili bean paste on the side.

Serves 4   Preparation time: 7 mins + 4 hours marinating time   Cooking time: 7 mins

Stewed Beef Ribs Galbi Jjim

2 lbs (1 kg) beef ribs, cut into bite-
  sized pieces
3–4 tablespoons soy sauce
2$\frac{1}{2}$ tablespoons rice wine or sake
2 teaspoons sesame oil
1 tablespoon sugar
6–8 cloves garlic, minced
2 spring onions, halved
$\frac{1}{2}$ teaspoon freshly ground black
  pepper
2 dried black Chinese mushroom,
  soaked in hot water for 30 minutes,
  stem discarded and cap sliced
1 small carrot, peeled and thickly
  sliced
14 oz (400 g) daikon radish (about
  6 in/15 cm), peeled and thickly
  sliced
4 dried chestnuts, soaked in hot
  water for 30 minutes
4 dried red dates
20 shelled gingko nuts

1 Rinse the ribs in cold water and drain. Bring a pot of water to a boil and cook the ribs for 10 minutes. Drain, then add enough water to the pot to just cover the ribs.
2 Add the soy sauce, rice wine, sesame oil, sugar, garlic, spring onions, black pepper and mushrooms, and bring to a boil. Cover, then reduce the heat to low and simmer gently for 30 minutes, or until the meat is tender.
3 Add the carrot, daikon, chestnuts, dried red dates and gingko nuts. Bring to a boil, then simmer over low heat for another 30 minutes, or until the vegetables are tender. Serve hot with rice.

Serves 4   Preparation time: 20 mins   Cooking time: 70 mins

Steamed Chicken with Ginseng   Dak Jjim

The chicken is best prepared using a pressure cooker, but it can also be simmered gently in a saucepan with a tight-fitting lid.

1 chicken (2 lbs/1 kg)
1²/₃ cups (400 ml) water
1 teaspoon salt
1 finger-thick piece fresh ginseng root
  or 2 tablespoons dried ginseng root

Stuffing
4 dried chestnuts, soaked in water
  for 30 minutes
4 baby potatoes (optional)
3 dried red dates
3 cloves garlic
1 slice ginger
¹/₂ teaspoon salt

1 Rinse the chicken inside and out, pat dry with paper towels and fill the cavity with the Stuffing. Close the cavity of the chicken by threading a skewer in and out of the flap.
2 Place the chicken in a pressure cooker and add the water, salt and ginseng. Close the cooker and bring up to pressure. Cook for 20 minutes, then reduce the pressure, but continue to cook the chicken for another 10 minutes until the meat is very tender. If using a pot, simmer tightly covered for 1 to 1¹/₄ hours, adding a little more water if the sauce evaporates. Ensure you turn the chicken several times during cooking to cook it evenly. Serve the chicken whole or cut into smaller serving pieces.

Serves 4   Preparation time: 15 mins   Cooking time: 30 mins

Spicy Chicken Stew   Dakdoritang

1 small chicken, cut into bite-sized
  chunks
2 cups (500 ml) water
4 small potatoes, quartered
1 large carrot, halved lengthwise,
  then cut into chunks
3 dried red dates
2 medium onions, thickly sliced
1 large leek, white part only, thinly
  sliced
2 green or red chilies, sliced diagonally and deseeded
2 teaspoons sesame oil
Sesame seeds, to garnish

Marinade
¹/₄ cup (60 ml) soy sauce
2 tablespoons chili bean paste
  (*gochujang*)
2–3 teaspoons ground red pepper

1 Heat a nonstick wok over medium heat and dry-fry the chicken pieces for 2 minutes. Set aside.
2 Place the ingredients for the Marinade in a medium-sized bowl and mix. Add the chicken, mix well and leave for 5 minutes.
3 In a large pot, add the chicken, Marinade and water, and bring to a boil. Cover, then reduce the heat and simmer for 15 minutes. Add the potatoes, carrot and dried red dates, and simmer for 20 minutes until tender, stirring several times.
4 Add the onions, leek and chilies, and simmer for 5 minutes. Drizzle the stew with the sesame oil, stir and remove from heat. Serve garnished with the sesame seeds.

Serves 4   Preparation time: 20 mins   Cooking time: 50 mins

Grilled Korean Beef Steak Chadolpakee

This recipe for grilled beef couldn't be easier. Start with thinly sliced good quality beef steak, grill it on a tabletop grill, and serve with sesame oil, salt and pepper, and a tangy Mustard and Lemon Sauce. The succulent, tender meat confirms the old saying that simple things in life are often the best.

1 teaspoon oil
4–8 cloves garlic, peeled and thinly sliced (optional)
1 lb (500 g) high quality beef sirloin, wrapped in plastic wrap, chilled in the
  freezer for 30 minutes, then thinly sliced
4 cloves raw garlic, to serve

Sesame Sauce
$1/_2$ tablespoon sesame oil
$1/_2$ tablespoon salt
$1/_4$ teaspoon freshly ground black pepper

Mustard and Lemon Sauce
2 teaspoons prepared Japanese or Chinese mustard
1 tablespoon brown sugar
1 teaspoon vinegar
4 teaspoons water
$2^1/_2$ tablespoons lemon juice

1 Combine the Sesame Sauce ingredients and set aside.
2 Combine the Mustard and Lemon Sauce ingredients and set aside.
3 Heat the oil in a nonstick skillet and add the sliced garlic. Stir-fry quickly for 30 seconds. Remove the garlic from the skillet and set aside.
4 Place the beef slices in a hot nonstick skillet or on a tabletop grill, and quickly sear it on 1 side. Turn the meat over and quickly sear on the other side. Serve the grilled meat with the Sesame Sauce, Mustard and Lemon Sauce, and both roasted and raw garlic.

Note: Koreans love to eat raw garlic with their meat. This quick and easy recipe is also commonly used to prepare grilled beef tongue, a Korean delicacy. Mustard and Lemon Sauce is an excellent accompaniment to any grilled meat.

Serves 4   Preparation time: 15 mins + 30 mins freezing time   Cooking time: 5 mins

Spicy Stir-fried Pork   Jeyookbokeum

A dish so tasty, your guests will never guess just how quick and easy it is to prepare.

1 lb (500 g) pork fillet or pork belly, thinly sliced
1 tablespoon vegetable oil
8 fresh shiitake mushrooms or 5 dried black Chinese mushrooms, rinsed, soaked in water for 30 minutes to soften, stems discarded and caps sliced
1 small onion, thinly sliced
1 leek, sliced
$1/2$ cup (100 g) kimchi, lightly squeezed dry and thinly sliced
2 red chilies, sliced diagonally
1 small green bell pepper, sliced into thick strips
Toasted sesame seeds, to garnish (optional)

Meat Marinade
3–4 tablespoons chili bean paste (*gochujang*)
1–2 teaspoons ground red pepper
2 cloves garlic, minced
1 teaspoon grated ginger
2 teaspoons sesame oil
1 tablespoon rice wine or sake
$1^{1}/_{2}$ tablespoons soy sauce
1 tablespoon sugar
2 tablespoons water

1 Combine the Meat Marinade ingredients in a medium bowl, stirring until the sugar is dissolved. Add the pork and mix to coat well. Drain the pork and reserve the marinade.

2 Heat the vegetable oil in a wok over high heat and stir-fry the pork for 1 minute. Add the mushrooms, onion, leek and kimchi, and stir-fry for another minute. Add the reserved marinade and continue to stir-fry until the pork is cooked, about 4 minutes.

3 Add the chilies and bell pepper, and stir to mix well. Sprinkle the sesame seeds and serve hot, with plenty of steamed rice.

Note: Although not traditionally Korean, add a small carrot and zucchini or sugar snaps in step 2 for a one-dish meal.

Serves 4   Preparation time: 15 mins   Cooking time: 5 mins

Pan-fried Chicken Skewers   Dakkochi Gui

1 lb (500 g) chicken thigh or breast
  fillets, cut into 24 pieces
1 clove garlic, crushed
$1/2$ teaspoon grated ginger
2 teaspoons sesame oil
$1/4$ teaspoon ground white pepper
16 small button mushrooms
8 spring onions or 2 leeks, white portion only, cut into 24 pieces
8 bamboo skewers
2 tablespoons vegetable oil

1 portion Bulgogi Marinade (page 78)

1 Prepare the Bulgogi Marinade by following the instructions on page 78.
2 Season the chicken pieces with the garlic, ginger, sesame oil and pepper.
Mix well and set aside to marinate for 5 minutes.
3 Thread 3 pieces of chicken, 2 pieces of mushrooms and 3 lengths of
spring onions alternately through a skewer. Repeat with the remaining ingredients, alternating them in the above order.
4 Coat the skewered ingredients with the Bulgogi Marinade and leave to
marinate for 5 minutes. Drain the marinade from the skewers into a small
saucepan and bring to a boil for 2 to 3 minutes, then pour the marinade
into 4 dipping bowls.
5 Heat the oil in a skillet and pan-fry the skewers over medium heat. Cook
for 2 to 3 minutes on each side, using a spatula to press down on the
skewers gently. If preferred, the skewers can also be placed under a grill or
broiler. Serve with the bowls of warmed Bulgogi Marinade.

Makes 8 skewers   Preparation time: 35 mins   Cooking time: 5 mins

Beef and Vegetable Skewers   Sanjeok

1 lb (500 g) beef sirloin, cut into
  24 pieces
8 oz (250 g) mushrooms (shiitake,
  button, winter or pine), stems discarded and caps thickly sliced
1 small red or green bell pepper
8 spring onions, white portion only,
  or 4 asparagus spears
8 long bamboo skewers
2 tablespoons vegetable oil

1 portion Bulgogi Marinade (page 78)

1 Prepare the Bulgogi Marinade by following the instructions on page 78.
2 Cut the beef, mushrooms, bell pepper and spring onions into roughly the
same size.
3 Thread pieces of beef, mushroom, bell pepper and spring onion or
asparagus through a bamboo skewer until all the ingredients are used up.
4 Place the skewers in a dish, coat with the Bulgogi Marinade and leave to
marinate for 10 minutes. Shake the excess marinade from the skewers.
5 Heat the oil in a skillet and pan-fry the skewers, pressing down gently with
a spatula for 5 minutes on each side, until the beef is cooked through.
Alternatively, place the skewers under a grill or a broiler.

Makes 8 skewers   Preparation time: 20 mins + 10 mins marinating time
Cooking time: 10 mins

Stir-fried Kimchi with Pork Belly or Beef
Dubu Kimchi

This is an appetizing, quick and easy dish, ideal for a simple meal with rice and perhaps a bowl of light soup. Sliced pork or beef is quickly stir-fried with kimchi, leek and garlic. Tofu is served warm, the final touch and the perfect accompaniment to this tangy, spicy kimchi stir-fry. The soft and creamy tofu adds both flavor and nutrition to this meal.

8 oz (250 g) pork belly, beef fillet or sirloin, thinly sliced
1 teaspoon vegetable oil (if using beef)
2 cups (500 g) sour kimchi, tightly packed, squeezed gently,
   and sliced into 1–in ($2^1/_2$–cm) pieces
$1/_2$–1 tablespoon ground red pepper
1 red chili, thinly sliced (optional)
1 teaspoon sugar
1 teaspoon minced garlic
1 leek, upper green portion only, thinly sliced
$1/_2$ teaspoon sesame oil
$1/_2$ teaspoon toasted sesame seeds (optional)

Warm Tofu
10 oz (300 g) firm tofu, cut into bite-sized pieces
Toasted black sesame seeds, to garnish

1 Stir-fry the pork belly in a dry wok for 3 minutes (the natural oil rendered from the pork belly should be sufficient). If using beef, heat the vegetable oil in a wok and stir-fry the beef over high heat until it changes color.
2 Add the kimchi, red pepper, chili, sugar, garlic and leek, and stir-fry for 1 minute. Reduce the heat to medium and cook for 7 minutes, stirring from time to time until the meat has absorbed the flavor of the kimchi. Remove from the heat and add the sesame oil and sesame seeds.
3 Prepare the Warm Tofu by placing the tofu in a mesh basket with a long handle and carefully lowering it into a pot of boiling water. Cook for 30 seconds to heat through (longer if using tofu directly from the refrigerator), then drain.
4 Place the stir-fried pork belly in the center of a serving plate and surround with pieces of tofu. Garnish the tofu with the black sesame seeds and serve with rice.

Note: A sour kimchi is best for this dish as the juice is absorbed into the meat and vegetables. You may need to adjust the amount of ground red pepper used, depending on the spiciness of the prepared kimchi.

Serves 4   Preparation time: 10 mins   Cooking time: 10 mins

Grilled Eel   Jangeo Gui

1 fresh eel, (about 2 lbs/1 kg),
  filleted
Bamboo skewers
Oil, to grease

1 portion Seafood Glazing Sauce
  (page 25)

Garnish
2 spring onions, green part only,
  thinly sliced
1 in (2$^1\!/_2$ cm) ginger, slivered
4 cloves garlic, sliced and grilled
$^1\!/_2$ tablespoon toasted sesame
  seeds
Ground white pepper

1 Prepare the Seafood Glazing Sauce by following the instructions on page 25.
2 To keep the eel fillets straight during cooking, gently thread the skewer through each fillet lengthwise. Heat a grill until very hot and brush the eel lightly with oil. Place the eel fillets on the grill, skin side away from the heat, and grill for 3 minutes on each side.
3 Brush one side of the eel with the Seafood Glazing Sauce and grill for a minute. Turn the eel over, brush the other side with the glazing sauce and grill for another minute. Repeat twice.
4 Cut the eel into 2$^1\!/_2$-in (6–cm) pieces. Garnish with the spring onions, ginger and garlic. Then sprinkle the sesame seeds and pepper. Serve hot.

Note: Eel can be bought parboiled or grilled, and vacuum packed from good Asian or Japanese markets. If eel is unavailable, salmon makes a good substitute.

Serves 4–6   Preparation time: 10 mins   Cooking time: 20 mins

Grilled Cod   Eundaegu Ganjang Gui

1 lb 3 oz (600 g) fresh cod, or other
  white fish fillets, cut into 4 pieces
Lemon slices, to serve

Marinade
$^1\!/_2$ cup (125 ml) water
1 tablespoon rice wine or sake
3 tablespoons soy sauce
1 tablespoon sugar or corn syrup
2 teaspoons lime or lemon juice
$^1\!/_2$ teaspoon sesame oil

1 Prepare the Marinade by mixing all the ingredients together. Pour it over the fish fillets, coating them well. Leave to marinate for 5 minutes. Pour the Marinade into a small saucepan and simmer, stirring constantly until it forms a light syrupy sauce. Keep warm.
2 Grill the fish under a hot grill for 3 to 4 minutes on each side, or until cooked. The grilling time may be longer, depending on the thickness of the fish. Transfer to a serving dish and spoon a little hot Marinade over the fish. Serve with the lemon slices.

Serves 4–6   Preparation time: 10 mins   Cooking time: 10 mins

Grilled Red Snapper   Okdom Gui

1 fresh red snapper fillet, or other
  white fish fillet (about 1$^1\!/_4$ lbs/600 g)
$^1\!/_2$ tablespoon salt
2–3 teaspoons sesame oil
Lemon slices, to serve
Fresh sprigs of parsley, to garnish

1 Rinse the fillet and pat it dry with paper towels. Sprinkle the fish on both sides with the salt and refrigerate for 30 minutes. Rinse briefly, then pat dry again.
2 Brush both sides of the fish generously with sesame oil and grill under a hot grill for 5 minutes on each side until cooked. Serve with the lemon slices and garnish with a few sprigs of the parsley.

Note: Alternatively, instead of grilling, you can pan-fry the fish in a hot skillet with $^1\!/_2$ tablespoon of sesame oil and 1 tablespoon vegetable oil.

Serves 4–6   Preparation time: 5 mins + 30 mins marinating time
Cooking time: 10 mins

Stir-fried Spicy Squid   Ojing-oh Bokeum

Simple to prepare and guaranteed to please.

3 medium squid (about $1^1/_2$ lbs/700 g), sliced into strips
  or 1 lb (500 g) boiled octopus, sliced into strips
3 tablespoons vegetable oil
1 small onion, very thinly sliced
3 cloves garlic, minced
$^1/_2$ teaspoon grated ginger
1–2 green chilies, cut into strips
  or $^1/_2$ bell pepper, cut into strips
8 shiitake or button mushrooms, stems discarded and caps sliced
1 small carrot, cut into strips (optional)
$^1/_2$–1 tablespoon chili bean paste (*gochujang*)
$1^1/_2$ tablespoons soy sauce
$1^1/_2$ tablespoons ground red pepper
$1^1/_2$ tablespoons sugar
1 teaspoon salt
1 teaspoon sesame oil
Toasted sesame seeds, to garnish

1 Heat the oil in a wok and add the onion, garlic and ginger, and stir-fry over high heat for about 30 seconds. Add the squid, chilies, mushrooms, carrot and chili bean paste, and stir-fry for 2 minutes, or until the squid turns white and is just cooked. Do not overcook or the squid will become tough.
2 Add the soy sauce, ground red pepper, sugar, salt and sesame oil. Mix well and garnish with the sesame seeds.

Note: If squid is unavailable, substitute with boiled octopus. Freshly cooked octopus is sold in Japanese and Korean specialty stores. To prepare fresh squid, remove the heads. If using, cut the tentacles just above the eyes and push out, and discard the hard, beaky portion in the centre. Cut the tentacles into sections. Remove the ink sac carefully and discard. Peel the skin and cut the squid into long rectangular strips. Rinse and pat the squid dry with paper towels.

Serves 4   Preparation time: 30 mins   Cooking time: 3 mins

Honey-drizzled Rice Cakes   Hwajeon

1³/₄ cups (220 g) rice flour
¹/₂ teaspoon salt
1 cup (250 ml) warm water
¹/₄ cup (60 ml) vegetable oil
¹/₄ cup (60 ml) honey
12 flower blossoms (such as azaleas, daisies or chrysanthemums), rinsed and dried, or toasted sesame seeds, to garnish

1 Mix the rice flour, salt and water to form a smooth, pliable but non-sticky dough. Tear off about 1 tablespoon of the dough and roll it out onto a lightly floured surface to make a circle, about 2¹/₄ in (6 cm) in diameter. Alternatively, transfer the dough to a floured surface and roll it out until it is about ¹/₂ in (1 cm) thick and use a cookie cutter or a drinking glass to cut out small circles of dough.
2 Heat the oil, over medium to high heat, swirling the skillet to cover the surface. When the oil is hot, place several pieces of the dough in the skillet. Reduce the heat and fry the rice cake for 2 to 3 minutes until golden brown underneath. Turn the rice cake over and cook on the other side for a minute. Drain on paper towels, then place the rice cakes on a serving plate and drizzle with honey. Garnish each rice cake with a flower blossom or the sesame seeds.

Makes 12 pieces   Preparation time: 15 mins   Cooking time: 15 mins

Persimmon Sherbet   Yeonci

When in season, persimmons turn from yellow to a beautiful red color. The tree loses all its leaves, while still bearing the fruits—creating a beautiful effect. This refreshing, all-natural dessert tastes like a sweet, soft, chilled custard, a soothing effect.

4 fresh, ripe but firm persimmons

1 Wash each persimmon, then wipe it dry. Freeze them overnight until they become solid. Serve the persimmons whole, or quarter each persimmon and serve the quarters individually on small plates.

Serves 4   Preparation time: 3 mins + overnight freezing

Korean Festive Cakes Songpyeon

These traditional cakes made of rice flour contain a variety of fillings—chopped sweetened chestnuts, sesame seeds or mung beans. This recipe uses slightly savory mung beans. If available, place the cakes on a bed of pine needles when steaming so that the delicious aroma imparts a subtle flavor to the cakes.

$1^1/_2$ cups (180 g) glutinous rice flour
$1/_4$ teaspoon salt
$3/_5$ cup (155 ml) water
$1/_2$ teaspoon sesame oil (optional)

Mung Bean Filling
$1/_3$ cup (70 g) split mung beans, simmered in $1/_4$ cup (60 ml) of water until soft, then drained
1 teaspoon sugar
$1/_4$ teaspoon salt

1 To make the Mung Bean Filling, mix the mung beans thoroughly with the sugar and salt, then set aside.
2 Sift the flour and the salt into a bowl and gradually add enough water to make a smooth, non-sticky dough. If the dough seems too wet to work with, add a little more rice flour. If desired, add a few drops of food coloring to color the dough. Knead the dough for 10 to 15 minutes.
3 Break off 1 tablespoon of dough and roll it into a ball. Flatten slightly, then press the center of the dough with your thumb to make a dent. Use your thumb and index finger to shape the dough into a Chinese teacup, pressing the dough lightly between your fingers and rotating the dough at the same time so that all the sides of the teacup are of even thickness. Place a heaped teaspoon of the filling into the cup, patting it down gently. Press the edges of the dough together to seal, pinching lightly to form a ridged seam. The filled dough should resemble a half moon. Repeat until all the dough and filling are used up.
4 Brush a plate with the sesame oil and place the cakes on the plate in a single layer. Steam for 30 minutes, or until the cakes are cooked. If desired, brush the top of each cake with the sesame oil, then serve warm, or at room temperature.

Note: Mung Bean Filling is savory. For a sweeter filling, use $1/_2$ cup (90 g) steamed chestnuts mashed with 2 teaspoons sugar. Always adjust amount of sugar in the recipe to taste.

Makes 10 cakes   Preparation time: 20 mins   Cooking time: 30 mins

Ginger Cookies Dipped in Honey   Yak Kwa

These unusual cookies are made from a pastry-like dough in which sesame oil replaces butter and the subtle flavoring is provided by fresh ginger juice, honey and rice wine. The deep-fried cookies are dipped in a sugar and honey syrup, and sprinkled with cinnamon and pine nuts. Serve them warm and watch them disappear quickly.

2 in (5 cm) ginger
1$^{1}/_{2}$–2 tablespoons water
2 cups (300 g) flour
Pinch of salt
3 tablespoons sesame oil
3 tablespoons honey
2 tablespoons rice wine or sake
Oil for deep-frying
Ground cinnamon (optional)
1 tablespoon crushed pine nuts (optional)

Syrup
$^{1}/_{2}$ cup (125 ml) water
$^{1}/_{4}$ cup (50 g) sugar
$^{1}/_{4}$ cup (60 ml) honey
Pinch of salt

1 Place the Syrup ingredients in a saucepan and bring to a boil, stirring frequently. Simmer for 1 minute, then remove from the heat.
2 Blend the ginger and water in a processor or spice grinder, then mash and strain to obtain the ginger juice. Set aside.
3 Place the flour and salt in a bowl and drizzle the sesame oil. Rub the oil into the flour mixture with your fingertips until the mixture resembles fine breadcrumbs. Add the ginger juice, honey, rice wine and enough water to make a pliable dough.
4 Turn the dough out onto a lightly floured board, then roll it out to a thickness of $^{1}/_{4}$ in (5 mm). Use a cookie cutter to cut the dough.
5 Heat the oil in a wok over very low heat and deep-fry the cookies slowly, a few at a time, until cooked and golden brown, about 2 to 3 minutes. If the oil is too hot, the cookies will brown before they are cooked through. Drain on paper towels, then use tongs to dip the cookies in the Syrup. Sprinkle the cinnamon and crushed pine nuts, if using.

Makes 40 cookies   Preparation time: 10 mins   Cooking time: 15 mins

Ginseng Tea   Insam-Cha

Ginseng is Korea's most famous product, a medicinal root whose amazing properties have been known for around 5,000 years.

10 whole pieces of dried ginseng root
4 dried red dates
8 cups (2 liters) water
3 tablespoons sugar, or more to taste
1 tablespoon pine nuts

1 Place the ginseng, dried red dates and water in a large saucepan. Bring to a boil, cover, then reduce the heat to low and simmer gently for 4 hours.
2 Add the sugar and stir to dissolve. Strain and serve in glasses or porcelain teacups, with a few of the pine nuts floating on the top.

Note: Top quality, whole, aged Korean ginseng root is very expensive. Packets of young, creamy white, dried rootlets and shavings (available in Chinese medicine shops and most Asian stores) are moderately priced and ideal for this recipe.

Serves 4   Preparation time: 5 mins   Cooking time: 4 hours

Persimmon Tea   Sujeonggwa

1 cinnamon stick (4 in/10 cm)
1¹/₂ in (4 cm) ginger, thinly sliced
4 black peppercorns
4 dried red dates
6 cups (1¹/₂ liters) water
3 tablespoons sugar, or more to taste
8 dried persimmons, soaked in water for 30 minutes, then drained (diced, if desired)
12 pine nuts

1 Place the cinnamon stick, ginger, peppercorns, dried red dates and water in a large saucepan and bring to a boil. Cover, then reduce the heat and simmer for 1 hour.
2 Add the sugar to taste and stir until dissolved. Pour the mixture through a sieve into a bowl and add the dried persimmons. Allow to cool, then refrigerate until well-chilled. When serving, pour the liquid into 4 bowls or glasses and add some of the pine nuts and a whole dried persimmon (or diced persimmon) to each serving.

Serves 4   Preparation time: 5 mins + 30 mins soaking time   Cooking time: 1 hour

Rice and Malt Tea   Sikhye

¹/₂ cup (125 g) malt, washed and drained
6 cups (1¹/₂ liters) water
4 tablespoons cooked rice
5 thin slices ginger
4 tablespoons sugar, or more to taste
12 pine nuts

1 Place the malt and water in a saucepan and bring to a boil. Cover, then reduce the heat and simmer very gently for about 45 minutes. Strain, discard the malt, and reserve the water.
2 Add the rice to the strained malt water, cover, and set aside in a warm place until the rice floats, about 3 to 4 hours.
3 Strain and reserve the liquid, then rinse the rice grains under running water. Place the rice grains in a covered container and refrigerate.
4 Bring the strained liquid to a boil with the ginger and sugar, stirring several times. Simmer for 10 minutes, then discard the ginger, cool and refrigerate the liquid. To serve, pour the tea into bowls or glasses and top with some of the chilled rice grains and the pine nuts.

Serves 4   Preparation time: 15 mins   Cooking time: 1 hour

Measurements and conversions

Measurements in this book are given in volume as far as possible. Teaspoon, tablespoon and cup measurements should be level, not heaped, unless otherwise indicated. Australian readers, please note that the standard Australian measuring spoon is larger than the UK or American spoon by 5 ml, so use a $^3/_4$ tablespoon instead of a full tablespoon when following the recipes.

Liquid Conversions

Imperial	Metric	US cups
$^1/_2$ fl oz	15 ml	1 tablespoon
1 fl oz	30 ml	$^1/_8$ cup
2 fl oz	60 ml	$^1/_4$ cup
4 fl oz	125 ml	$^1/_2$ cup
5 fl oz ($^1/_4$ pint)	150 ml	$^2/_3$ cup
6 fl oz	175 ml	$^3/_4$ cup
8 fl oz	250 ml	1 cup
12 fl oz	375 ml	$1^1/_2$ cups
16 fl oz	500 ml	2 cups
32 fl oz	1 liter	4 cups

Note:
1 UK pint = 20 fl oz
1 US pint = 16 fl oz

Solid Weight Conversions

Imperial	Metric
$^1/_2$ oz	15 g
1 oz	28 g
$1^1/_2$ oz	40 g
2 oz	55 g
3 oz	85 g
$3^1/_2$ oz	100 g
4 oz ($^1/_4$ lb)	110 g
5 oz	140 g
6 oz	170 g
7 oz	200 g
8 oz ($^1/_2$ lb)	225 g
9 oz	250 g
10 oz	300 g
16 oz (1 lb)	450 g
32 oz (2 lbs)	900 g
36 oz ($2^1/_4$ lbs)	1 kg

Oven Temperatures

Heat	Fahrenheit	Centigrade/Celsius	British Gas Mark
Very cool	225	110	$^1/_4$
Cool or slow	275-300	135-150	1-2
Moderate	350	175	4
Hot	425	220	7
Very hot	450	230	8

Index of recipes

Mail-order/online sources

The ingredients used in this book can all be found in markets featuring the foods of Southeast Asia. Many of them can also be found in any well-stocked supermarket or Korean specialty store. Ingredients not found locally may be available from the mail-order and online sources listed below.

AsianWok.com
www.asianwok.com

Anzen Importers
736 NE Union Avenue
Portland, OR 97232
Tel: 503-233-5111

Central Market
40th and North Lamar
Austin, TX 78756
Tel: 512-206-1000
www.centralmarket.com

Dekalb World Farmers Market
3000 East Ponce De Leon
Decatur, GA 30034
Tel: 404-377-6401
www.dekalbfarmersmarket.com

Dean & Deluca
560 Broadway (Prince St)
New York, NY 10012
Tel: 212-226-800
www.deandeluca.com

EthnicGrocer.com
www.ethnicgrocer.com

Gourmail, Inc.
816 Newton Road
Berwyn, PA 19312
Tel: 215-296-4620

HanAhReum Asian Mart
1720 Route 70 E.
Cherry Hill, NJ 08003
Tel: 856-489-4611
www.hanahreum.com
(Korean language website)

ikoreaplaza.com
www.ikoreaplaza.com

Kam Man Food Products
219 Quincy Avenue
Quincy, MA 02169-6754
Tel: 212-755-3566
www.kammanfood.net

KoaMart
www.koamart.com

Nancy's Specialty Market
P.O. Box 327
Wye Mills, MD 21679
Tel: 800-462-6291

Oriental Food Market and Cooking School
2801 Howard Street
Chicago, IL 60645
Tel: 312-274-2826

Oriental Market
502 Pampas Drive
Austin, TX 78752
Tel: 512-453-9058

Pacific Mercantile Company, Inc.
1925 Lawrence Street
Denver, CO 80202
Tel: 303-295-0293
www.pacificmercantile.com

Uwajimaya
600 5th Ave South, Suite 100
Seattle, WA 98104
Tel: 206-624-6248
www.uwajimaya.com

Wasabi
10194 SW Parkway
Portland, OR
Tel: 503-292-1861